APPROACHING THE BENCH FROM INSIDE THE IMMIGRATION COURT

WILLIAM K. ZIMMER

AuthorHouse™ LLC
1663 Liberty Drive
Bloomington, IN 47403
www.authorhouse.com
Phone: 1-800-839-8640

© 2013 William K. Zimmer. All rights reserved.

No part of this book may be reproduced, stored in a retrieval system, or transmitted by any means without the written permission of the author.

Published by AuthorHouse   08/08/2013

ISBN: 978-1-4817-2908-6 (sc)
ISBN:978-1-4817-2907-9 (hc)
ISBN: 978-1-4817-2906-2 (e)

Library of Congress Control Number: 2013905143

This book is printed on acid-free paper.

Because of the dynamic nature of the Internet, any web addresses or links contained in this book may have changed since publication and may no longer be valid.

The views expressed in this work are solely those of the author and do not necessarily reflect the views of the publisher, and the publisher hereby disclaims any responsibility for them.

Table of Contents

Dedication vii

Quotation From *The Federalist*, No. 31 ix

Introduction.. xi

Chapter I — History of the Immigration Court 1

Chapter II — Removal Proceedings..29

Chapter III — Persecution and Torture Claims..............................41

Chapter IV — Hardship Claims.. 65

Chapter V — Legitimation of Immigration Status 91

Chapter VI — Marriage Fraud Amendments 105

Chapter VII — Waivers..119

Chapter VIII — Voluntary Departure 165

Chapter IX — Bond Hearings 175

Chapter X — Motions to Reopen and Motions to Reconsider.... 183

Conclusion 189

Quotation From *Midsummer's Night Dream*, Act V, Scene 2 195

Dedication

This book is dedicated to the private immigration attorneys, the INS and DHS attorneys and the immigration court law clerks whose hard work, preparation, patience and integrity have enlightened me and enabled my work as an Immigration Judge.

I will forever be grateful for the solid support provided by the immigration court clerical staff in Miami, Florida and Houston, Texas, in spite of heavy workloads and limited staffing.

Finally, words alone fall short of expressing the appreciation and respect that I have acquired for interpreters who labor to capture the colloquy of the courtroom upon which the record of proceedings is founded. The integrity of the record created through professional and competent interpreters is truly a measure of the integrity of our immigration courts.

. . .Men, upon too many occasions, do not give their own understanding fair play; but, yielding to some untoward bias, they entangle themselves in words and confound themselves in subtleties. . .

Alexander Hamilton
The Federalist, No. 31

Introduction

At a modest gathering of immigration attorneys in Houston, Texas on the occasion of my retirement from the immigration court bench, several members of the group stood up to speak in the tradition of retirement parties. It was gratifying to share memories about their professional experiences involving me during my days on the bench. Among the various stories (including an infamous crime against nature involving a horse and whether it was a crime involving moral turpitude) and poignant sometimes tearful accounts of various clients who had been granted asylum, cancellation of removal, a waiver or adjustment of status, curiosity was expressed about the "black book" that had been observed in use on my bench. The purpose for the following pages is to partially pierce the veil of mystery about the immigration court, to provide a better understanding about immigration court proceedings and the culture of government institutions that implement and enforce immigration law, and to throw in my two cents worth of an opinion here and there. With this purpose in mind, the "black book" observed on my bench is used as the format for subject matter relating to law and procedure. I hasten to note, mindful of those zealous ethics attorneys in the Executive Office For Immigration Review ("EOIR") Office of the General Counsel, that, although the EOIR maintains a general "Bench Book" for reference by Immigration Judges, the "black book" described above has no connection whatsoever to the official EOIR "Bench Book." My "black book" is entirely my own work product, derived from personal experience and original sources.

I have also included some anecdotal humor comprised primarily of excuses for criminal behavior submitted during immigration proceedings for the purpose of justifying such behavior. To appreciate some of this material it is necessary to be equipped with a dark sense of humor. I have found that levity in small increments, even when related to serious matters, can help people survive in a stressful work environment. Most immigration hearings end with tears of sorrow or tears of joy without much middle ground. *See Stress and Burnout Found Among Nation's Immigration Judges*, a study conducted at the University of California, San Francisco, published in the Georgetown Immigration Law Journal [Vol. 23:57; 2008]. In addition, the excuses provide insight about the thought processes of all human beings. We all seek justification for our behavior based on our social nature. Almost everyone is familiar with the adage: "There is honor, even among thieves." Some rationales for criminal behavior are more sophisticated than others, but the goal is the same in all of them; justification of behavior to appear socially acceptable. Thus, each excuse, regardless of credibility, is a plea for empathy founded on presumed universal moral principles. I have often asked myself how I would behave in the circumstances surrounding other individuals' unlawful behavior, and have concluded that the best way to avoid trouble is to avoid the occasion of trouble. I intend no disrespect or disparagement of any group or individual. The excuses for criminal behavior are not set forth for the authors to be judged or ridiculed. They are included for humorous content and they create the feel of what it is like to apply the law in immigration court by providing a human context. Our immigration law and institutions are all about people. The material relating to the excuses is derived from notes taken during my hearings and transcripts as well as written communications, but it is taken out of context. More information is needed to properly assess the credibility and merit of the excuses. Finally, the excuses for criminal behavior provide insight about the application of criminal law and sometimes illustrate criminal law concepts (e.g. the meaning of "possession," as applied to contraband, intentional and knowing conduct, reckless conduct, negligent conduct, inchoate crimes, the law of parties, etc.).

Given the nature of this work, it seems appropriate to issue a caveat. This book is not intended to be an academic treatment of immigration law and procedure, especially since I am more of a carpenter than an architect. Anyone who is familiar with immigration law knows that immigration law evolves quickly and continuously with the ebb and flow of many currents and counter currents in our political environment, as well as the unfolding of national and international events. Therefore, case citations are mostly restricted to water shed cases or cases that illustrate or explain a legal principle or standard. Even this limited use of references is subject to obsolescence in time. The march toward obsolescence of legal standards in the realm of immigration law is not always neat and orderly or linear. Sometimes, chimerical creatures composed of the old and the new appear before our eyes, like the questing beast sought by King Pellinor in Arthurian legend. Who would have guessed, for example, that after the passage of the Illegal Immigration Reform and Immigrant Responsibility Act of 1996 ("IIRIRA") in which Congress substituted the term, "Entry," with a definition of "admission" and "admitted" in section 101(a)(13) of the Immigration and Nationality Act that the United States Supreme Court would continue to cling to the old "Entry" doctrine for lawful permanent residents returning to the United States from abroad? *See Vartelas v. Holder*, 132 S. Ct. 1479, 566 U.S. ___ (2012).

In short, this book is intended for laymen and lawyers alike who have an interest in the business that our immigration courts conduct and, to a limited extent, the manner in which our immigration courts and the Department of Homeland Security conduct that business. Finally, at the risk of tedium by repetition, the work that follows is not intended to be comprehensive or authoritative and is more accurately classified as random information and opinion than legal research.

CHAPTER 1

History of the Immigration Court

Lengthy labels seem to characterize agencies charged with administering immigration matters. For example, the immigration court currently resides in The Executive Office For Immigration Review ("EOIR"), a subdivision of the Department of Justice. Try typing this title on an address label without acronyms.

The government entity having immigration responsibilities has been moved about in the federal government, almost like an unwanted step-child. Congress created the position of "Superintendent of Immigration" in the Treasury Department in 1891 which appears to be the very beginning of the former Immigration and Naturalization Service. *See* section 7 of the Act of March 3, 1891. The function of the "Superintendent of Immigration" was transferred from the Treasury Department to the Department of Commerce and Labor in 1903. *See* section 22 of the Act of March 3, 1903. In 1913, the immigration function and the naturalization function were designated as separate bureaus in the newly created Department of Labor. *See* section 551 of the Act of March 4, 1913. In 1933, Franklin D. Roosevelt, with Congressional approval, directed the consolidation of the immigration and naturalization bureaus into the Immigration and Naturalization Service of the Department of Labor. *See* Executive Order No. 6166 of June 10, 1933. It was not until 1940 that the Immigration and Naturalization Service was transferred to the Department of Justice in accordance with the "Hoover Plan." *See* the Reorganization Act of 1939. EOIR, home to the immigration court and the Board of Immigration Appeals ("BIA"), had evolved in the Immigration and Naturalization Service until EOIR emerged as an independent agency in 1983. Finally, in 2002 Congress abolished the former Immigration and Naturalization Service and transferred its operating units to the newly formed Department of Homeland Security ("DHS") as Immigration and Customs Enforcement ("ICE") and Citizenship and Immigration Services ("CIS"). *See* Homeland Security Act, Pub. L. 107-296, 116 Stat. 2135 (2002). These dual operating units are reminiscent of the bifurcated bureaus of Immigration and Naturalization Services that had previously resided in the Department of Labor. Congress, however, preserved the EOIR in the Department of Justice. Thus, the immigration court survived the 2002 transfer of the Immigration and Naturalization Service functions to the DHS and currently remains in the Department of Justice.

Before offering my opinion about the evolution and culture of the immigration court, it is appropriate to outline my experience with immigration inspection and other processes. Hopefully, a brief personal history will provide insight to the reader about my point of view. In 1972, I worked as an employee of the Detroit and Canada Tunnel Corporation as a tunnel guard. The Tunnel Company issued me a badge, a flashlight and a hard hat to carry out my duties of directing traffic and periodically patrolling, on foot, the Detroit Windsor Tunnel for blockages or delays caused by traffic incidents and accidents, or any other anomalies. Tunnel guards were expected to ensure orderly lines of traffic leading to the inspection booths and to request the opening of inspection lanes from Customs and Immigration offices. These offices were located across the traffic lanes from each other. At that time, the Department of Treasury employed customs inspectors and the Department of Justice employed immigration inspectors. The customs office resided on the side of the inspection booths closest to the Detroit River near Randolph Street. The immigration office was located above the customs office on a rise between the inspection booths and Jefferson Avenue on the southern side of Detroit. It might be of interest to some readers to note that a curious twist of geography places Windsor, Canada south of the United States and Canada border. Sometimes, the opening of new inspection lanes in response to increased traffic volume provoked minor verbal skirmishes between the customs crews and the immigration crews when the immigration office lacked sufficient personnel to open a new lane in its turn, especially on a cold winter day. The Customs Service always seemed to have more resources than the Immigration Service. This perception is consistent with the natural impression one might expect an ordinary observer to form, since the Treasury Department generally collects money and the Department of Justice does not. Regardless of the truth regarding disparate resources of the two services, the perception of officers in the field created its own reality. This perception about uneven resources was further strengthened in the minds of immigration and customs officers by the more remunerative reimbursable overtime provisions enjoyed by customs officers under the 1911 Act Governing Overtime. Reimbursable overtime for immigration officers was provided under the Act of March 2, 1931. The above description of the resource disparity is a digression, but the reader was warned in the introduction about random information. Returning to the duties of tunnel guards, when immigration officers rejected aliens applying for admission, the tunnel guards were responsible for escorting the rejected person or persons back to Canada. This was accomplished by walking with rejected pedestrian(s) to the tunnel bus that traveled back and forth in the tunnel between Canada and the United States. The tunnel guard was expected to verify that the rejected alien boarded the bus and that the bus departed. If the rejected person or persons had been traveling by automobile the tunnel guard lowered a chain and directed the driver into the traffic lane heading back to Canada through the tunnel. These escort duties were performed by Detroit and Canada Tunnel Corporation employees because the proprietor of the tunnel was subject to the same laws and regulations that applied to carriers such as aircraft and vessels arriving in the United States from abroad. If for some reason an automobile or a pedestrian evaded inspection or return to Canada after denial of admission to the United States by an immigration officer the Detroit Windsor Tunnel Corporation was fined $500 for each person involved in the violation.

The Customs Service hired me as a customs inspector in 1974. At that time, customs inspectors were cross-designated immigration inspectors through training for the purpose of primary border inspection. I worked at the Detroit Windsor Tunnel and the Ambassador Bridge, a second designated international port of entry in Detroit, performing border inspections of people and vehicles coming to the United States from Canada. Upon transferring to Houston, Texas, in 1978, I worked at the Houston Intercontinental Airport, the Houston Hobby Airport and the Houston ship channel. Airport duties in Houston at that time were divided between passenger inspection terminals, airline cargo facilities and other warehouses. At the Houston Hobby Airport, private aircraft and some commercial cargo aircraft were inspected, usually by a single inspector. If aliens were on board the aircraft an immigration officer was also assigned in the discretion of the immigration officer in charge of the port of entry. When a ship arrived at the Port of Houston from abroad, an immigration officer and a customs officer boarded the ship. The customs officer who boarded the ship would obtain the manifest from the ship's captain. Customs officers ultimately compared unladed cargo from the ship with cargo listed on the manifest. Customs officers were assigned to supervise the unlading of ships and to inspect cargo, such as oil well casing and steel and other cargo for which immediate release had been sought by the importer. For oil and chemical tankers, customs officers measured the product on the ship before and after unlading and also gauged the shore tank(s) before and after unlading. The immigration officer would inspect the crew and passengers if any and determine whether to admit crew and passengers by issuing an Arrival Departure Record

(Form I-94). Any person not admitted would be confined on board the ship which was the responsibility of the ship's captain. As you can see, the Customs Service is oriented to control *things* that come into the United States by inspecting them and collecting tariffs. The Immigration Service is oriented to control *people* arriving in the United States through the inspection process.

My first employment as a licensed attorney occurred in 1985 as Assistant District Attorney in the 9th Judicial District of Montgomery County, Texas. I worked in intake, drafting and presenting indictments to the Grand Jury, as well as drafting complaints to obtain arrest and search warrants, and took part in five criminal trials. While I was working as an Assistant District Attorney, Congress passed the Immigration Reform and Control Act of 1986 ("IRCA"). This legislation not only contained amnesty provisions for the legalization of aliens (including agricultural workers) who had been continuously present in the United States after illegally entering the United States as of 1982, employer sanctions for knowingly hiring aliens without work authorization and increased border enforcement. IRCA also provided for the hiring of immigration trial attorneys. Although I enjoyed working for the Montgomery County District Attorney's Office, I applied for re-employment by the federal government as an immigration trial attorney. Ultimately, I was hired by the former Immigration and Naturalization Service ("INS") as a trial attorney in 1987 and assigned to the Houston, Texas litigation unit. Before I was hired as a trial attorney, there were only two government immigration trial attorneys in Houston. At the same time, however, three Special Inquiry Officers (now entitled Immigration Judges) presided in Houston. This required the infant Houston litigation unit to decide which courts would *not* be attended by a trial attorney. If an immigration investigator was available he or she would be assigned to represent the INS in the immigration court that lacked a trial attorney. *See* 8 C.F.R. § 242.9(a) [1987] (providing for assignment of an additional immigration officer to perform the duties of a trial attorney). Current regulations require assignment of a government attorney when the removal charge is contested or is not conceded and when an unrepresented alien in immigration proceedings is incompetent or under 18 years of age. In all other circumstances, assignment of a government attorney is optional. *See* 8 C.F.R. § 1240.2(b).

Houston trial attorneys were not only assigned to immigration court for exclusion, deportation and rescission proceedings. Sometimes a trial attorney would appear in state criminal court or submit a brief in state criminal court to present the INS position regarding a Judicial Recommendation Against Deportation ("JRAD"). If the state court judge issued a JRAD in a criminal proceeding, the offense for which the alien was convicted could not be used to frame an exclusion or deportation charge to justify initiating immigration court proceedings, except for drug convictions and foreign convictions. Trial attorneys sometimes explained to state court judges that a conviction does not absolutely mandate deportation. For example, if the offense for which the alien was convicted is a petty offense issuing a JRAD would diminish the defendant's incentive for rehabilitation because the INS would not be able to combine the offense with a subsequent offense to justify future deportation or exclusion proceedings. Trial attorneys would sometimes explain that the defendant would have an opportunity to present equities that would be weighed against adverse factors in immigration court if a waiver was available, or that the defendant could qualify for other relief from deportation in the absence of a JRAD. I can't recall any Houston case in which the INS did not oppose the issuance of a JRAD. As of November 29, 1990, Congress repealed the JRAD provision by enacting section 505 of the Immigration Act of 1990, Public Law No. 101-649. However, JRADs issued before November 29, 1990 must still be honored. This is another detail for immigration attorneys to remember, whose clients established a criminal history before the JRAD repeal date. Given the expanding definition of "Aggravated Felony" under section 101(a)(43) of the Immigration and Nationality Act, as amended ("the Act"), as well as the seemingly increasing risk that ICE will brand an offense with the nebulous stamp of disapproval (i.e. crime involving moral turpitude ("CIMT")) some immigration attorneys would probably applaud the return of JRADs.

Houston trial attorneys also handled employer sanctions litigation before the Office of the Chief Administrative Hearing Officer ("OCAHO") in EOIR. This type of litigation involved discovery under the Federal Rules of Civil Procedure, such as interrogatories and depositions, which I can only describe as time consuming. Employer sanctions cases in Houston also attracted a significant amount of media attention, and INS headquarters considered them to be sensitive. Trial attorneys were instructed not to talk to the media about employer sanctions or any other subject.

The Houston INS litigation unit assigned a trial attorney to the U.S. Attorney's Office as a Special Assistant United States Attorney ("SAUSA"). The SAUSA would assist the representation of the INS and the Department of Justice ("DOJ") in civil and criminal cases. However, the INS, not the United States Attorney's Office, paid the SAUSA's salary. Inevitably, this assignment involved responding to writs of habeas corpus and other motions relating to immigration matters filed in U.S. District Court.

Trial attorneys were also assigned to represent the INS in Merit System Protection Board ("MSPB") cases. These cases involved controversies between the agency and an employee. *See* 5 U.S.C. Part III and 5 C.F.R. Part 1201. *See Douglas v. Veterans Administration*, 5 M.S.P.B. 313; 5 M.S.P.R. 280 (1981).

Finally, Houston trial attorneys provided legal advice to operating units, but operating units were not required to follow legal advice from the local litigation office. Acceptance of legal advice depended on the officer and his or her supervisor. Many of the requests seemed to come from deportation officers who would inquire about motions to reopen before deporting an alien. Investigators involved in employer sanctions enforcement would usually communicate well with the assigned trial attorney. Sometimes, investigators would seek advice about search and seizure. Occasionally, trial attorneys would receive inquiries from examination officers and supervisory inspectors, but almost never from any other unit. There was no requirement for operating units to seek legal advice in the ordinary course of business, even if it involved initiating exclusion, deportation, or rescission proceedings.

This brings me to an opportunity to offer an opinion about the evolution of the immigration court and how the system could be improved to ensure independent decision making and fundamental fairness. Legislative history and the collective experience of customs officers and immigration officers relating to the processing of aliens arriving in the United States from abroad strongly suggests that the creature we know as the immigration court evolved out of the inspection process. The inspection process in the context of this book is the face to face interaction between an international traveler seeking admission to the United States and a government officer or surrogate.

After passage of the notorious Alien Sedition Acts of 1798 which expressly expired two years after enactment and the almost forgotten Naturalization Act of 1798, Congress did not pass any significant immigration related legislation until after the American Civil War. It might be interesting to some readers to note that the Naturalization Act of 1798 not only required registration of aliens for the first time in United States history. The Naturalization Act of 1798 made naturalization almost impossible. Congress repealed the provisions of the Naturalization Act of 1795 which required 5 years of residence in the United States and a declaration of intent to become a United States citizen 3 years before naturalization. Under the new provisions of the Naturalization Act of 1798, an applicant for naturalization was required to declare an intention to become a United States citizen 5 years before naturalization; prove 14 years residence in the United States; and prove registration that had to be maintained throughout the entire 14 year period by re-registration upon each arrival in the United States. Perhaps, this restrictive change in law reflected fear of foreign influence during a dangerous time in United States history. Tensions between the United States and France were running high during John Adams' presidency, after war had been declared between Britain and France in 1793. It seems that the interest of current day politicians in the political leanings of immigrant groups is nothing new.

Congress specifically addressed the inspection process in section 8 of the Act of March 3, 1891. The language of this section of law is provided as follows:

> That upon the arrival by water at any place within the United States of any alien immigrants it shall be the duty of the commanding officer and the agents of the steam or sailing vessel by which they came to report the name, nationality, last residence, and destination of every such alien, before any of them are landed, to the proper inspection officers, who shall thereupon go or send competent assistants on board such vessel and there inspect all such aliens, or the inspection officers may order a temporary removal of such aliens for examination at a designated time and place, and then and there detain them until a thorough inspection is made. But such removal shall not be considered a landing during the pendency of such examination. The medical examination shall be made by surgeons of the Marine Hospital Service. In cases where the services of a Marine Hospital Surgeon can not be obtained without causing unreasonable delay the inspector may cause an alien to be examined by a civil surgeon and the Secretary of the Treasury shall fix the compensation for such examination. *The inspection officers and their assistants shall have power to administer oaths, and to take and consider testimony touching the right of any such aliens to enter the United States, all of which shall be entered of record. . . All decisions made by the inspection officers or their assistants touching the right of any alien to land, when*

adverse to such right, shall be final unless appeal be taken to the superintendent of immigration, whose action shall be subject to review by the Secretary of the Treasury. . .[Emphasis Added]

That the Secretary of the Treasury may prescribe rules for inspection along the borders of Canada, British Columbia, and Mexico so as not to obstruct or unnecessarily delay, impede, or annoy passengers in ordinary travel between said countries: *Provided*, That not exceeding one inspector shall be appointed for each customs district, and whose salary shall not exceed twelve hundred dollars per year.

All duties imposed and powers conferred by the second section of the act of August third, eighteen hundred and eighty-two, upon State commissioners, boards, or officers acting under contract with the Secretary of the Treasury shall be performed and exercised, as occasion may arise, by the inspection officers of the United States. . .

In section 2 of the Act of August 3, 1882, referenced in the last paragraph quoted above, Congress had empowered the Secretary of the Treasury to enter into contracts with state commissions, boards, or officers designated by the state governors "to take charge of the local affairs of immigration in the ports within said State . . ." These entities and officers were authorized to appoint other persons to carry out immigration responsibilities and reported in writing any passenger found to be a "convict, lunatic, idiot, or any person unable to take care of himself or herself without becoming a public charge" to the customs collector of the port, and such persons were not permitted to land.

Clearly, after passage of the Act of March 3, 1891, the inspection process was no longer carried out by officers appointed by the above described state entities, but by inspection officers of the United States. This transfer of duties from nonfederal agencies to the federal government appears similar to the transfer of airport security

APPROACHING THE BENCH FROM INSIDE THE IMMIGRATION COURT

processing to the Transportation Security Administration in more recent times. The emphasized language quoted above describes a process familiar to participants in current immigration court proceedings; the taking of sworn testimony entered of record and the right of appeal to a higher authority. Also noteworthy is the inspector's delegation of authority to assistants whose determinations could be reviewed by the superintendent of immigration and ultimately by the Secretary of the Treasury. Only one inspector was permitted in each district, so it seems likely that the inspector would rely on appointed assistants to inspect passengers and review the work of the assistants before an appeal was forwarded to a higher level. Probably, a hierarchy of junior and senior assistants soon developed. It is apparent that all appeals arising from the inspection process described in the Act of March 3, 1891 stayed in the same executive agency that denied the alien's application for admission; the United States Treasury Department.

The inspection process that was transferred to federal officers in 1891 has remained in place to this day. The actual person to person interaction between an applicant for admission at a port of entry and a federal officer, in spite of technological advances, characterizes the current inspection process. Any international traveler can verify this personal aspect of border inspection. The inspection process is significant because the role of the Immigration Judge grew out of it. Knowledge about the origins of the immigration court cultivates an understanding of the immigration court itself and the way that is perceived by federal immigration enforcement agencies such as ICE and its litigation units.

The inspection process was very important to the implementation of early immigration laws because control of immigration was exclusively asserted through the exercise of exclusion authority. A student of history might point out that the Act of June 25, 1798 provided for deportation:

That it shall be lawful for the President of the United

States at any time during the continuance of this act, to order all such aliens as he shall judge dangerous to the peace and safety of the United States, or shall have reasonable grounds to suspect are concerned in any treasonable or secret machinations against the government thereof, to depart out of the territory of the United States . . .

However, as noted earlier in this chapter, the Act of June 25, 1798 expired 2 years after enactment. Thus, the power to deport aliens, as opposed to the power to exclude aliens did not exist for practical purposes in United States immigration law until after 1880.

Congress provided for the exclusion of prostitutes and convicts in section 3 of the Act of March 3, 1875, but did not provide for the deportation of aliens (except for Chinese persons found in the United States in violation of Chinese exclusion provisions in the Act of May 6, 1882) until 1891. The Chinese exclusion provisions resulted from a treaty with China dated November 17, 1880. *See* section 12 of the Act of May 6, 1882 (repealed by the Act of December 17, 1943). In section 11 of the Act of March 3, 1891, Congress provided for the removal of excludable aliens within 1 year of arrival. The time period during which an excludable alien could be apprehended and removed from the United States expanded to 2 years (for aliens found to be a public charge) and 3 years for other aliens found in the United States in violation of law. *See* sections 20 and 21 of the Immigration Act of March 3, 1903. Being excludable at the time of arrival was the foundation for all of these early deportation provisions.

Congress also provided for *Special Inquiry Boards* in 1903. In section 24 of the Act of March 3, 1903, describing the duties of *Immigrant Inspectors*, Congress provided that:

. . .The decision of any such officer, if favorable to the admission of any alien, shall be subject to challenge by any other immigration officer, and such challenge shall operate to take the alien whose right to land is so challenged before a board of special inquiry for its investigation. Every alien who

APPROACHING THE BENCH FROM INSIDE THE IMMIGRATION COURT

may not appear to the examining immigrant inspector at the port of arrival to be clearly and beyond a doubt entitled to land shall be detained for examination in relation thereto by a board of special inquiry.

In section 25 of the Act of March 3, 1903, Congress provided:

That such boards of special inquiry shall be appointed by the commissioners of immigration at the various ports of arrival as may be necessary for the prompt determination of all cases of aliens detained at such ports under the provisions of law. Such boards shall consist of three members, who shall be selected from such of the immigrant officials in the service as the Commissioner-General of Immigration, with the approval of the Secretary of Commerce and Labor, shall from time to time designate as qualified to serve on such boards: *Provided*, That at ports where there are fewer than three immigrant inspectors, the Secretary of Commerce and Labor, upon recommendation of the Commissioner-General of Immigration, may designate other United States officials for service on such boards of special inquiry. Such boards shall have authority to determine whether an alien who has been duly held shall be allowed to land or be deported. All hearings before boards shall be separate and apart from the public, but the said boards shall keep complete permanent records of their proceedings and of all such testimony as may be produced before them; and the decision of any two members of a board shall prevail and be final, but either the alien or any dissenting member of said board may appeal through the commissioner of immigration at the port of arrival and the Commissioner-General of Immigration, to the Secretary of Commerce and Labor, whose decision shall then be final; . . .

Apparently, these boards of inquiry were typically made up of three immigration inspectors who were charged with investigating the admissibility of an alien who had not been found "to be clearly and beyond a doubt entitled to land." Not only could a favorable decision to admit an alien be challenged at a port of entry by any other immigration officer, but a favorable decision by a board of special inquiry could be appealed by one dissenting board member.

The following extract from *Brief Statement of the Investigations of the Immigration Commission, with Conclusions and Recommendations and Views of the Minority, Reports of the U.S. Immigration Commission (1911)* provides insight about how Congress viewed boards of special inquiry approximately 7 years after creating them:

> Boards of special inquiry are one of the most, if not the most, important factor in the administration of the immigration law. To them are referred for decision all cases held by the examining surgeon because of disease or mental or physical defects, and also every alien who may not appear to the examining immigrant inspector to be clearly and beyond doubt entitled to land. In the case of aliens certified by the examining surgeon as being afflicted with a loathsome or dangerous contagious disease, tuberculosis, or pronounced mental defects, the board has no alternative but to exclude, and from its decision in such cases there is no appeal. In the case of persons held as contract laborers or because of the likelihood that they may become a public charge, and in other cases, the board exercises discretionary power as to the admission or rejection of the alien, in which cases, however, there lies the right of appeal to the Secretary of Commerce and Labor. The boards exercise a power which if not properly used may result in injustice to the immigrant or, through the admission of undesirable aliens, in harm to the country. It is important, therefore, that these boards should be composed of unprejudiced men of ability, training, and good judgment. . . . At all the important ports the boards of special inquiry

APPROACHING THE BENCH FROM INSIDE THE IMMIGRATION COURT

are composed of immigrant inspectors, who are generally without judicial or legal training. This, together with the fact that they are selected by the commissioners of immigration at the ports where they serve, tends to impair the judicial character of the board and to influence its members in a greater or less degree to reflect in their decisions the attitude of the commissioner in determining the cases. The character of their decisions is indicated somewhat by the fact that nearly 50 per cent of the cases appealed are reversed by the Secretary of Commerce and Labor, whose decision, under the law, must be based solely upon the evidence adduced before the board. This record of reversals on appeal suggests that their decisions which are not reviewed may be equally wrong.

In justice to the immigrant, and to the country as well, the character of these boards should be improved. They should be composed of men whose ability and training fit them for the judicial functions performed, and the provision compelling their hearings to be separate and apart from the public should be repealed. . .

Clearly, the above observations and recommendations of the U.S. Immigration Commission in 1911 reflect concern about the quality and integrity of the inspection process and awareness of the need for a judicial approach to making decisions about the admission and exclusion of aliens applying for admission to the United States. These boards of special inquiry continued to function after Congress transferred immigration and naturalization services to the Department of Justice in 1940. *See* the Reorganization Act of 1939; section 1 of the Reorganization Plan No. V (effective June 4, 1940).

When I was working as an Immigration Judge in Miami, Florida, EOIR participated in a pilot program with the former INS in 1996. The pilot program involved the physical presence of an Immigration Judge at the Miami International Airport for the purpose of immediately holding exclusion hearings for aliens who wanted such a hearing. Holding the exclusion hearing at the airport avoided detention of the applicant in a detention facility while awaiting the hearing. It was very much like traveling back in time to the beginning of the 20th century. During the time that I presided over exclusion hearings at the Miami International Airport, not many applicants for admission asked for a hearing. Eventually, the pilot program expired and, to my knowledge, never emerged again.

It was not until Congress passed the Immigration and Nationality Act of June 27, 1952 ("the 1952 Act"), that the board of special inquiry was replaced by a solitary special inquiry officer, defined as follows:

> The term "special inquiry officer" means any immigration officer who the Attorney General deems specially qualified to conduct specified classes of proceedings, in whole or in part, required by this Act to be conducted by or before a special inquiry officer and who is designated and selected by the Attorney General, individually or by regulation, to conduct such proceedings. Such special inquiry officer shall be subject to such supervision and shall perform such duties, not inconsistent with this Act, as the Attorney General shall prescribe.

See section 101(a)(4) of the 1952 Act.

The authority and duties of a special inquiry officer are described in section 242(b) of the 1952 Act as follows:

> A special inquiry officer shall conduct proceedings under this section to determine the deportability of any alien, and shall administer oaths, present and receive evidence, interrogate, examine, and cross-examine the alien or witnesses, and, as authorized by the Attorney General, shall make determinations, including orders of deportation. . .
> In any case or class of cases in which the Attorney General

APPROACHING THE BENCH FROM INSIDE THE IMMIGRATION COURT

believes that such procedure would be of aid in making a determination, he may require specifically or by regulation that an additional immigration officer shall be assigned to present the evidence on behalf of the United States and in such case such additional immigration officer shall have authority to present evidence, and to interrogate, examine, and cross-examine the alien or other witnesses in the proceedings. Nothing in the preceding sentence shall be construed to diminish the authority conferred upon the special inquiry officer conducting such proceedings. No special inquiry officer shall conduct a proceeding in any case under this section in which he shall have participated in investigative functions or in which he shall have participated (except as provided in this subsection) in prosecuting functions. . .

Congress, in the same section, provides for the promulgation of regulations to establish safeguards for the alien using the following language:

> . . .Such regulations shall include requirements that –
> (1) The alien shall be given notice, reasonable under all the circumstances, of the nature of the charges against him and of the time and place at which the proceedings will be held;
> (2) The alien shall have the privilege of being represented (at no expense to the Government) by such counsel, authorized to practice in such proceedings, as he shall choose;
> (3) The alien shall have a reasonable opportunity to examine the evidence against him, to present evidence in his own behalf, and to cross-examine witnesses presented by the Government; and
> (4) No decision of deportability shall be valid unless

> it is based upon reasonable, substantial, and probative evidence.

See section 242(b) of the Immigration and Nationality Act of 1952.

It appears that, after almost 50 years of experience with boards of special inquiry and keeping the concerns noted by the U.S. Immigration Commission in 1911 in mind, Congress substituted a single special inquiry officer for the more cumbersome 3-person board of special inquiry and provided specific safeguards for the alien. However, the notion that the special inquiry officer is a sort of investigative immigration officer, sometimes working in concert with another immigration officer, to present evidence, examine, and cross-examine witnesses, etc. is retained. This conjunction of different and sometimes divergent investigative and judicial functions created tension in performing the duties of a special inquiry officer that continues to this day for Immigration Judges. The description of the duties of an Immigration Judge in section 240(b)(1) of the Immigration and Nationality Act, as amended ("the Act") is essentially the same as the description of the duties of special inquiry officers in section 242(b) of the 1952 Act.

Commentary

The Executive Office For Immigration Review ("EOIR") containing the immigration courts and the Board of Immigration Appeals ("BIA") is the product of a Department of Justice reorganization that took effect on January 9, 1983. In my opinion, this attempt to separate the judicial function involving immigration controversies from the law enforcement and operational functions of the former INS was a laudable response to the tension between the investigative and judicial roles described above and the need to avoid the public appearance of the special inquiry officer as a rubber stamp. Before

APPROACHING THE BENCH FROM INSIDE THE IMMIGRATION COURT

EOIR was created, I had heard that the special inquiry officer, like other immigration officers was a subordinate of the INS district director who exercised administrative control over supplies, resources and facilities provided for the special inquiry officer in the district office. The district director was in a position to influence a special inquiry officer by reducing or withholding administrative resources, or by force of personality. I can't verify that this actually happened, but the administrative dependency and proximity of special inquiry officers to district directors as subordinate immigration officers did not make such influence impossible. The reader might recall that the U.S. Immigration Commission in 1911 expressed concern that officers comprising the boards of special inquiry were selected by the commissioner of immigration at the port where they serve, which tended to impair the judicial character of the board and to influence board members in a greater or less degree to reflect in their decisions the attitude of the commissioner. The potential for this sort of direct influence ended with the creation of EOIR in the DOJ. The insulation of EOIR from the influence of law enforcement and administrative influence of the former INS increased again with the dissolution of INS and the transfer of immigration law enforcement and immigration services to DHS in 2002.

Since EOIR is the product of agency reorganization, Congress did not have a hand in it. The reorganization, therefore, is laudable, but falls short of more complete independence for the immigration court that only Congress can provide. As a former customs officer, government attorney and Immigration Judge, I have observed the general attitude of enforcement personnel at various levels in the former INS, and more recently DHS attorneys in immigration court. Law enforcement is often competitive on various levels between agencies and individuals. As described above, subtle jealousies have existed over disparate overtime provisions provided by their respective agencies among customs and immigration inspectors. When I worked for the Customs Service, different grade levels existed among the customs inspectors. New customs officers were generally hired at a GS-5 pay level with automatic increases to GS-7 and ultimately the GS-9 journeyman inspector. Senior inspectors enjoyed GS-11 status. The Customs Service paid supervisory inspectors at the GS-12 level. Lower grade officers with a modicum of ambition would seek recognition for promotion by making seizures and taking enforcement actions. Some immigration officers took pride in "breaking" an alien, by persuading the alien to admit to some type of immigration violation. This was usually done by confronting the suspected violator with evidence available to the inspector during secondary examination.

A common attitude in the former INS and in the ICE litigation unit is an expectation hailing back to the description of the Special Inquiry Officer and Immigration Judge as an investigator or chief prosecutor, assisted by another government attorney. This attitude is not without foundation, but it exacerbates the tension between dual judicial and investigatory functions of the Immigration Judge. I have occasionally sensed an expectation of accommodation on the part of ICE in immigration court. As an Immigration Judge, I have responded to the question originating in the former INS litigation unit: "Isn't the purpose of the immigration court to enforce the immigration laws of the United States?" In my opinion, the general answer is "Yes," BUT in modern times, the primary purpose of the immigration court is to provide a forum that is fundamentally fair to the alien without interfering with the prosecutorial role of the ICE. One primary purpose for any court is to provide a neutral forum where the parties are procedurally on equal footing and where individuals enjoy due process of law. The immigration court does not have investigators or any means of conducting investigations. The Immigration Judge has no authority to require or control an ICE investigation. Investigative and prosecutorial duties are necessarily the primary responsibility of the ICE. The removal hearing itself is at best a very dull investigative tool. Unlike the special inquiry officer in the 19th and early 20th centuries when hearings were more closely linked with the inspection process, removal hearings often take place long after the inspection process or apprehension of the alien has occurred. No matter how many questions are asked of witnesses, there is usually no way to independently confirm or rebut the testimony in the hearing itself. Once the litigation unit receives a file from a DHS operating unit, it is extremely difficult for the government attorney to persuade the operating unit to produce additional evidence or to investigate further. Every Immigration Judge must integrate dual functions in carrying out his or her duties. Specific choices along the tension line between prosecutor and judge must be made in conducting removal hearings and issuing decisions. As outlined above, the historical trend for the immigration court has been in the direction of emphasizing the judicial role of the Immigration Judge as opposed to the prosecutorial and investigative role. The 1996 change of title from "special inquiry officer" to "Immigration Judge" is a reflection of this trend. Due to this trend toward a judicial role and the practical impediments to conducting investigations in immigration court at a greater distance in time and location from the inspection process (from which the role of Immigration Judge evolved) it appears that the best choice for the Immigration Judge is to emphasize the judicial role and fundamental fairness, leaving the investigative and prosecutorial duties in the hands of the DHS. This translates into procedurally treating the DHS and the respondent as litigants with equal footing in a neutral venue within the confines of the law. The law itself often favors the DHS by assigning the burden of proof to the respondent most of the time, especially when the respondent is an applicant for admission to the United States. *See* section 240(c)(2), (4) of the Act; 8 C.F.R. § 1240.8(b), (c), (d). The DHS, for example, is not limited by time and number bars governing motions to reopen. *See* section 240(c)(6), (7); 8 C.F.R. § 1003.23(b). I believe that the immigration court is more valuable in terms of fundamental fairness and creating public confidence in the integrity of its performance, as well as more efficient, when it is conducted by an Immigration Judge rather than a Special Inquiry Officer.

The only way to completely free the immigration court from

the influence of the executive arm of government that enforces immigration law as well as policies promulgated in the same executive arm of government is to take the immigration courts out of the DOJ and establish them as independent legislative courts. This would more effectively insulate the immigration court from influence of the executive arm of government. Congress, for example, converted the tax court from an administrative court to a constitutional court in the Tax Reform Act of 1969. Only Congress can do this by designating the immigration courts as legislative courts under Article I of the United States Constitution. Government agencies are generally averse to giving up jurisdiction or power. Also, arguments might be made that converting the immigration courts into constitutional courts would be inconsistent with the need for immigration proceedings to be expeditious. One answer to this argument is that immigration proceedings are no more efficient now than proceedings that can be anticipated in a constitutional legislative court. The parties in immigration court can now appeal to the BIA. From the BIA, the DHS can appeal to the Attorney General and the respondent can appeal to the Court of Appeals having jurisdiction over the trial court. Ultimately, the respondent can appeal to the United States Supreme Court, like any other litigant in the United States court system. In fact, converting the immigration court to a constitutional legislative court might make immigration proceedings more expeditious by eliminating the administrative review that is currently conducted by the BIA. If the immigration court became a constitutional legislative court immigration appeals could be taken directly to the circuit courts of appeal, thereby eliminating the time such appeals would otherwise remain pending before the BIA. Even if the number of immigration appeals remained the same, there would be one less layer of review before final disposition.

Before stepping down from my soap box, I believe there is a way to improve the manner by which immigration proceedings are initiated, regardless of whether or not the immigration courts should become constitutional legislative courts. The former INS did not and the DHS does not utilize government trial attorneys in the process by which immigration cases are filed for prosecution in immigration court. There is no procedure for the exercise of discretion by litigation units before a Notice to Appear ("NTA") (Form I-862) is filed in immigration court to initiate removal proceedings. The ICE litigation units conduct a perfunctory review aimed at catching drafting errors, but ICE litigation units cannot say no to an operating unit based on prosecutorial discretion. Criminal proceedings require an indictment signed by a grand jury foreman or an information signed by a prosecuting attorney. In criminal law proceedings, a law enforcement officer must present the results of an investigation to an intake unit in a state or federal prosecuting office to obtain a decision about whether or not the prosecuting office will prosecute the matter. Immigration litigation is civil by nature; not criminal. However, the stakes are high for those who are accused of being aliens who are subject to removal from the United States. In some ways, removal from the United States, although not technically punishment, is worse than serving a jail sentence. As noted by Supreme Court Justice Louis Brandeis, deportation from the United States can deprive a person of "life, or of all that makes life worth living." *See Ng Fung Ho v. White*, 259 U.S. 276, at 284 (1922). Presently, the law and regulations provide that laymen, not attorneys, issue NTAs to initiate immigration court proceedings. Governing regulations pursuant to 8 C.F.R. § 239.1(a) make this clear:

Issuance of notice to appear. Any immigration officer, or supervisor thereof, performing an inspection of an arriving alien at a port-of-entry may issue a notice to appear to such alien. In addition, the following officers, or officers acting in such capacity, may issue a notice to appear:

(1) District directors (except foreign);

(2) Deputy district directors (except foreign);

(3) Chief patrol agents;

WILLIAM K. ZIMMER

(4)   Deputy chief patrol agents;
(5)   Patrol agents in charge;
(6)   Assistant patrol agents in charge;
(7)   Field operations supervisors;
(8)   Special operations supervisors;
(9)   Supervisory border patrol agents;
(10) Supervisory border patrol agents;
(11) Service center directors;
(12) Deputy service center directors;
(13) Assistant service center directors for examinations;
(14) Supervisory district adjudications officers;
(15) Supervisory asylum officers;
(16) Officers in charge (except foreign);
(17) Assistant officers in charge (except foreign);
(18) Special agents in charge;
(19) Deputy special agents in charge;
(20) Associate special agents in charge;
(21) Assistant special agents in charge;
(22) Resident agents in charge;
(23) Supervisory special agents;
(24) Directors of investigations;
(25) District directors for interior enforcement;
(26) Deputy or assistant district directors for interior enforcement;
(27) Director of detention and removal;
(28) Field office directors;
(29) Deputy field office directors;
(30) Supervisory deportation officers;
(31) Supervisory detention and deportation officers;
(32) Directors or officers in charge of detention facilities;
(33) Directors of field operations;
(34) Deputy or assistant directors of field operations;
(35) District field officers;

APPROACHING THE BENCH FROM INSIDE THE IMMIGRATION COURT

(36) Port directors;

(37) Deputy port directors;

(38) Supervisory service center adjudications officers;

(39) Unit Chief, Law Enforcement Support Center;

(40) Section Chief, Law Enforcement Support Center; or

(41) Other officers or employees of the Department or of the United States who are delegated the authority as provided by 8 CFR 2.1 to issue notices to appear.

DHS policy does not authorize attorneys in DHS litigation units to decline prosecution. Aside from attempts to persuade an operating unit that a case should not be prosecuted, DHS attorneys are governed by the decision of the operating unit to pursue removal of an alleged removable alien in immigration court. Sometimes, once an NTA is issued and the case is transferred for prosecution, the originating office considers its work done and is reluctant to expend any more time or resources on it: It's off the desk for prosecution.

After an NTA is filed in immigration court, a DHS assistant chief counsel (or any of the above listed officers) can move for dismissal of an NTA under 8 C.F.R. § 1239.2(c) for one or more of 7 specific reasons as follows:

1) The respondent is a national of the United States;

2) The respondent is not deportable or inadmissible under immigration laws;

3) The respondent is deceased;

4) The respondent is not in the United States;

5) The Notice to Appear was issued for failure to file a timely petition under section 216(c) of the Act, but the untimely filing was excused under section 216(d)(2)(B) of the Act (i.e. excused for "good cause and extenuating circumstances");

6) The Notice to Appear was improvidently issued; or

7) Circumstances have changed after the Notice to Appear was issued to the extent that continued prosecution of a removal order is no longer in the best interest of the government.

See 8 C.F.R. § 239.2(a). Other than moving for dismissal, the only action permitted by a DHS assistant chief counsel is to amend the NTA by adding a lodged charge and/or changing the allegations. *See* 8 C.F.R. § 1240.10(e). As opposed to criminal proceedings, the charging instrument in immigration proceedings is issued without meaningful discretionary review by the litigation unit that has the responsibility to prosecute respondents in immigration court. Current regulations and practice are not structured to provide an effective filter for initiating immigration litigation that permits the exercise of prosecutorial discretion by DHS litigation units responsible for representing the DHS in immigration court. This appears to be one of the circumstances that set the stage for the politically charged controversy over the implementation of the 2012 DHS prosecutorial discretion policy. Review of immigration proceedings *after* such proceedings had been initiated without the meaningful exercise of prosecutorial discretion helped draw attention to the policy.

The law and regulations could be structured to better provide for meaningful legal review before initiating removal proceedings by doing away with the present system that allows only laymen to issue NTAs. NTAs should be issued by litigation units under the authority of a chief legal officer. A litigation unit should have the discretion to reject proposed cases that lack sufficient evidence, as well as cases that are not suitable for litigation. The immigration court might be a humble administrative court, but the record of proceedings in immigration court is subject to appellate review by the highest courts of our country, including the United States Supreme Court. For individuals confronted by the DHS and charged with being removable aliens, the immigration court is the door through which these individuals must pass, dragging with them the DHS as a litigant, to obtain review in the judicial branch of the United

States. For this reason alone, the DHS should not casually initiate immigration court proceedings without meaningful discretionary review by its prosecuting attorneys. Too much garbage can clog almost any drain. Litigating bad cases will often result in bad case law for the government.

CHAPTER II
Removal Proceedings

One way to describe a removal proceeding is to compare it to a criminal trial. Criminal trials are in two parts; the guilt phase and the punishment phase. Removal proceedings are also divided into two parts. In the first part, the Immigration Judge will determine whether the DHS allegations are true and support the removal charge and whether the removal charge can be sustained. In the second part of the proceedings, the respondent, whom the DHS has proven to be a removable alien, has the right to apply for relief from removal. Relief from removal usually takes the form of one or more applications to legitimate immigration status permanently or temporarily to avoid removal. Various applications for relief from removal will be discussed in greater detail later in this book.

During the course of a removal hearing, the respondent is entitled to a reasonable opportunity to obtain legal counsel at no expense to the federal government. This is not an absolute right to counsel. *See Vides-Vides v. INS*, 783 F.3d 1463, 1469 (9th Cir. 1986). The respondent also has the right to review and object to DHS evidence (except evidence involving the national security of the United States), to submit testimony and evidence and cross-examine witnesses. *See generally*, section 240(b)(4) of the Act. Removal proceedings are generally open to the public. *See* 8 C.F.R. § 1240.10(b).

The very first hearing in removal proceedings is described as a master calendar hearing. At the first master calendar hearing, the Immigration Judge will inform the respondent about the right to representation at no expense to the government, and provide a legal aid list of pro bono organizations in the city where the hearing is being conducted. In addition, the Immigration Judge will inform the respondent about the nature of removal proceedings and the respondent's rights in such proceedings. This involves describing in plain language the basic structure of removal proceedings, the allegations and removal charge(s), the respondent's rights, and making certain that the respondent understands. *See* 8 C.F.R. § 1240.10. The Immigration Judge will explain or provide written notice that if the respondent fails to appear at a removal hearing without exceptional circumstances outside of the respondent's control the respondent will be ordered removed from the United States in his or her absence. A removal hearing conducted in the respondent's absence is known as an *in absentia* hearing. The Immigration Judge will inform the respondent that if a removal order is issued in an *in absentia* hearing the respondent will become ineligible for a period of 10 years for voluntary departure, adjustment of status, cancellation of removal and an application known as registry. *See* section 240(b)(7) of the Act. This responsibility makes it very important for an Immigration Judge to be patient and strive to be a good communicator. A judicial temperament is sometimes more important than legal acumen, but hopefully these traits will go hand in hand. Usually, another master calendar hearing is scheduled to allow time for the respondent to consult and hire legal counsel if requested by the respondent. Law and regulations obligate the Immigration Judge to inform the respondent at some time during immigration proceedings about apparent eligibility for relief from removal. *Matter of Cordova*, 22 I&N Dec. 966, at 968 (BIA 1999). Even if the respondent is represented, Immigration Judges often engage the respondent's representative in a brief discussion about potential relief applications before scheduling a hearing on the merits of relief from removal.

EWI

Government Attorney: Did you go over this application with your attorney?
Respondent: Yes.

Government Attorney: Did you understand this application?
Respondent: Yes.

Government Attorney: Did you sign this application?
Respondent: Yes.

Government Attorney: Is this your signature on this application?
Respondent: Yes.

Government Attorney: If you were admitted to the United States as you testified why did you indicate "EWI" as your manner of entry on this application?
Respondent: I thought "EWI" meant everyone was inspected.

In the world of immigration, "EWI" is commonly used as an acronym for "entry without inspection." This is an example of how real or feigned ignorance of the jargon used by immigration professionals can frustrate cross examination based on the presumption that everybody is familiar with the same terminology.

The second part of removal proceedings is often described as a merits hearing or an individual hearing. At the conclusion of the merits hearing, the Immigration Judge will issue an oral decision containing findings of fact and conclusions of law and an order disposing of the respondent's relief applications. *See Matter of S-H-*, 23 I&N Dec. 462 (BIA 2002); *Matter of Rodriguez-Carrillo*, 22 I&N Dec. 1031 (BIA 1999). The oral decision distinguishes the work of Immigration Judges from their counterparts in other types of administrative and constitutional courts. The oral decision is a legal art form that permits a more efficient adjudication of high volume dockets if it is done well. Experience teaches that if an Immigration Judge regularly reserves decision in favor of issuing a written decision at a later date stacks of reserved decisions will quickly bury that Immigration Judge. Even a small army of law clerks (that doesn't exist in any immigration court) will not be able to rescue an Immigration Judge who does not learn the art of delivering oral decisions. An attorney with experience in state courts and federal district courts once commented to me that he had never heard a judge give such a thorough oral explanation for the disposition of a case as he had heard in immigration court. The topic of oral decisions reminds me of a true story told to me by a former colleague whom I followed into retirement. An immigration practitioner who frequently represented respondents in immigration court had become accustomed to losing most of his cases during a legal career that can only be described as less than illustrious. During one particularly long winded oral decision, this attorney fell asleep at the counsel table with his client sitting next to him. At the end of the oral decision the Immigration Judge granted the client's application and the INS trial attorney waived appeal. When the Immigration Judge routinely turned to the respondent's attorney to ask if he accepted the favorable decision, there was no response. The attorney's client understandably became anxious. The client did not speak English, and did not understand the outcome of his hearing. The Immigration Judge was looking in his direction and talking to his snoozing attorney. Finally, the client elbowed the attorney who spontaneously jumped to his feet and as a reflex announced that his client reserved his right to appeal. Upon realizing he had been victorious, the attorney withdrew his appeal and the decision became final. All's well that ends well. The notion of marketing some of my oral decisions as a cure for insomnia has occurred to me, but once delivered any proprietary rights if they ever existed are lost as part of the public record.

At the merits hearing, the respondent has the burden of proof, by preponderance of evidence to establish eligibility for relief from removal. *See* section 240(c)(4)(A) of the Act; 8 C.F.R. § 1240.8(d). *Matter of Acosta*, 19 I&N Dec. 211, at 215-16 (BIA 1985). The Immigration Judge will terminate removal proceedings if the DHS cannot establish the removal charge by clear and convincing evidence. *See* section 240(c)(3) of the Act; 8 C.F.R. § 1240.8(a). The assignment of burden of proof and persuasion regarding removal charges is not always clear, especially when it involves a charge of presence without admission or a compound charge involving an exclusion ground or a lawful permanent resident alien returning from abroad. *See* section 240(c)(2) of the Act. *See Vartelas v. Holder*, 132 S. Ct. 1479, 566 U.S. ___ (2012). Of course, the DHS must always establish alienage by clear and convincing evidence before any removal charge can be sustained.

When a derivative citizenship claim (i.e. citizenship derived from birth abroad to one or more United States citizen parents) is involved, respondents sometimes fall short of proving derivative citizenship by a preponderance of evidence in an application for a certificate of citizenship (Form N-600). *See* section 341 of the Act; 8 C.F.R. § 341.2(c). It is not uncommon for this situation to develop due to the unavailability of witnesses and evidence (i.e. the death of one or more parents, faded memories, or the lack of documentation or other evidence of retention requirements). Retention requirements refer to various required time periods of a United States citizen parent's physical presence in the United States (depending on the law in effect at the time of the applicant's birth) as a condition for derivative citizenship of the offspring. Typically, part of the retention period must have occurred after the United States citizen parent reached a specified age. For example, the retention requirement for derivative citizenship under section 322(a)(2) of the Act is as follows:

> (2) The United States citizen parent –
> (A) has (or at the time of his or her death had) been physically present in the United States or its outlying possessions for a period or periods totaling not less than five years, at least two of which were after attaining the age of fourteen years. . .

Nevertheless, in immigration proceedings the DHS must establish alienage by clear and convincing evidence. The DHS benefits as a litigant from the presumption of alienage arising from birth outside the United States. *See, for example, Matter of A-M-,* 7 I&N 332 (BIA 1956); *Matter of Tijerina-Villarreal,* 13 I&N Dec. 327 (BIA 1969); *Matter of Ponco,* 15 I&N Dec. 120 (BIA 1974); *Matter of Vergara,* 15 I&N Dec. 388 (BIA 1975). The respondent, however, might be able to rebut the presumption of alienage arising from birth abroad by presenting a preponderance of evidence to establish his or her derivative citizenship claim before an Immigration Judge. The Immigration Judge is not bound by the decision of the DHS and will consider the derivative citizenship claim *de novo* (legalese meaning a new decision unaffected by a previous decision).

While the subject of citizenship by birth is still fresh, a real life story about a United States citizenship claim in immigration court seems appropriate. One of my fellow retired Immigration Judges told me about a *pro se* respondent (a respondent who is representing himself or herself) who insisted that he was a United States citizen by birth. The Immigration Judge had explained to him that there were only two ways to obtain United States citizenship; by birth or naturalization. The government trial attorney perfunctorily submitted a Mexican birth certificate relating to the respondent

APPROACHING THE BENCH FROM INSIDE THE IMMIGRATION COURT

who enthusiastically pulled out a *baptismal* record from a small town in Texas and declared "But I was born again in the United States!" The Immigration Judge calmly replied "Let's talk about the first time you were born."

Other proceedings conducted by Immigration Judges are as follows: deportation hearings, exclusion hearings, bond hearings for eligible detained aliens, credible fear hearings, reasonable cause hearings, rescission hearings, asylum only hearings and withholding only hearings.

Removal Proceeding Participants

Participants in removal proceedings include the respondent, the respondent's attorney if the respondent is represented, the Immigration Judge, the DHS attorney, an interpreter conversant in English and the language that the respondent best speaks and understands and sometimes an EOIR legal assistant, especially for master calendar hearings.

The DHS attorney is a licensed attorney. Many are experienced and very knowledgeable about immigration law and court procedure. The DHS attorney represents the position of the DHS in immigration court. DHS attorneys, however, do not have the same relationship with their client (the DHS) as an attorney who is representing a respondent in removal proceedings. For practical purposes, the DHS is the DHS attorney's employer, rather than a client. The DHS provides salary and employee benefits and does not allow its attorneys to practice law in the private sector. Consequently, the DHS dictates policy and severely limits the exercise of professional judgment by its attorneys. I enjoyed much more freedom to exercise discretion as a state prosecutor, than as an INS trial attorney. I have heard jocular remarks about the limited use of discretion by federal government attorneys, such as "You need permission to go to the restroom." Private sector attorneys who are representing clients in immigration court should keep in mind that, even if a DHS attorney agrees with you about a legal position, he or she might not be able to express agreement in court. The DHS posture on legal issues is generally dictated by policy makers at higher levels who ordinarily are not privy to the unique and various circumstances that surround individual respondents. This exemplifies some of the frustrations of dealing with the government. Sometimes it seems that nobody can make a decision. Also, the government will be around long after the present generation has turned to dust. Consequently, the government does not share the same time constraints with individuals who must conduct business with it. Waiting 2 or 3 years for the government to make a decision or take some ministerial action might profoundly affect an individual who has a limited time to live, but it has no significant impact on the government or its agents. For those readers who would like to explore this subject matter, I suggest reading *The Facts in the Great Beef Contract* by Mark Twain. Here is an excerpt:

"...Young man, why didn't the First Comptroller of the Corn-Beef Division tell me this?"

"He didn't know anything about the genuineness of your claim." "Why didn't the Second tell me? Why didn't the Third? Why didn't all those divisions and departments tell me?"

"None of them knew. We do things by routine here. You have followed the routine and found out what you wanted to know. It is the best way. It is the only way. It is very regular, and very slow, but it is very certain."

"Yes, certain death..."

One of the valuable qualities of the Immigration Judge for individuals confronted by the DHS in immigration litigation is the relative independence of the Immigration Judge from the policy driven postures of the DHS regarding legal issues. The Immigration

APPROACHING THE BENCH FROM INSIDE THE IMMIGRATION COURT

Judge still enjoys more independence than DHS attorneys with regard to the interpretation of the law as it applies to the facts of cases within the jurisdiction of the immigration court. I sometimes hear comments from the private immigration bar urging uniformity among the Immigration Judges with regard to procedure and interpretation. Beware what you ask. If you want uniformity the government is likely to give it to you in overabundance. To the extent that the independence of the Immigration Judges in interpreting and applying immigration law is limited, the value of the immigration court is undermined. Sometimes, the immigration court serves as a buffer between the respondent and inflexible policy driven law enforcement and operational arms of the DHS. The government naturally is inclined toward uniformity, as noted above with regard to the limited discretion of DHS attorneys. The federal government is a titanic litigant in terms of power and resources and time compared to an individual. Occasionally, it behaves like a steam roller by rolling over and crushing deviations from the norm, rather than addressing them. The result is a flat hard uniform policy. Uniform policy is always favored in a bureaucracy, because it reduces the need for decision making. Just follow the policy. However, as most of us know, flexibility is necessary to meaningfully address unique situations that characterize the human condition. As an appendage of an executive agency, the immigration court is not a cure, but at least it can provide some pain relief within the limits of its independence. It appears that, due to increased supervisory oversight of Immigration Judges, introduced by former Attorney General Alberto Gonzalez in 2008, agency mission goals (such as case completion goals), joint projects with the DHS (such as sharing reset codes in the EOIR computer for purposes of work authorization adjudications by the DHS) and an expanding operating procedures manual, etc., the immigration court is drifting in the direction of a uniform policy driven entity like any other federal government agency. In other words, the cumulative effect of supervising Immigration Judges (sometimes by supervisors with little or no experience as an Immigration

Judge), pressure to conform to administrative agendas and EOIR management coordination with the DHS (a party to immigration court proceedings) is the erosion of independent decision making by Immigration Judges. These pressures are arguably appropriate in a federal executive agency, but appear to be inappropriate for the health of a court system charged with independent decision making and nurturing fundamental fairness.

The essential participant in immigration proceedings who is often taken for granted is the interpreter. To gain insight about the function of an interpreter, try watching or listening to a news broadcast. Repeat in the same language, without interpretation, exactly what is being said, either simultaneously or consecutively. Chances are that you will soon be stumped. Repeating exactly what is being said is what interpreters are expected to do during a removal hearing, except the interpreters are converting one language to another. Since translation, rather than interpretation, is the goal in court proceedings, the title, "interpreter," seems to be a misnomer. Interpreters do not enjoy the luxury of improving or altering the form or content of statements. Attorneys should strive to simplify questions as much as possible. Keep it short and sweet and you'll not only be appreciated by the interpreter, but you'll leave a clear record for future briefing and appellate review.

The legal assistant is another unsung hero behind the scenes of the immigration court. When I was in Miami, an ongoing joke evolved regarding the unending stream of motions filed in immigration court. In Miami, my clerk and I privately joked about dividing motions filed in my court into two categories. The motions would be classified by asking one question: "Does this make work for the clerk?" If the answer was "yes," the motion was declared denied in jest. This was an inside joke, and motions were NEVER actually adjudicated based on the "work for the clerk" test. Litigants and Immigration Judges should try to make everything as clear and as simple as possible to ensure efficient and accurate data entries. For example, litigants should file forms such as change of address forms and notices of appearance using the standard blue and green colored paper, respectively, rather than submitting copies of the same forms on white copy paper. Not only is this required in the Immigration Court Practice Manual, but compliance reduces the risk that the forms will be overlooked or lost in a file full of other white sheets of paper. The Immigration Court Practice Manual sets forth in detail how to file anything that is relevant to removal proceedings. Just follow the instructions. Litigants should use conventional terminology to describe motions. Standard terminology can be found in the Immigration Court Practice manual. All of this makes life easier for the legal assistant who won't have to puzzle over how to classify the motion. Finally, timely filings reduce work for the clerk who will not need to pull the file for review by the Immigration Judge or annotate the file as "late." Most filings in immigration court are time sensitive. Specific time lines for just about everything are set forth in the Immigration Court Practice Manual, and Immigration Judges can set specific deadlines. *See* 8 C.F.R. § 1003.31(c). An immigration practitioner once explained to me that his filing was late because he ran out of time working to meet an overwhelming number of deadlines. I couldn't help reminding him that, according to Einstein's special theory of relativity, the faster you go the slower time passes for you. So if he worked faster he would have more time. He just gave me a blank look (which I deserved). Luckily, his untimely filing was not fatal in that particular situation. In short, attention to detail and timeliness will make life easier for the legal assistant, and anything immigration court participants can do to make life easier for the legal assistant will make life easier for everybody. Finally, in spite of the frustrations and pressures of practicing law or working in a bureaucracy, attorneys and Immigration Judges should always behave courteously when interacting with EOIR clerical staff.

CHAPTER III

Persecution and Torture Claims

Asylum

An applicant for asylum in the United States must qualify as a refugee within the meaning of section 101(a)(42)(A) of the Act. *INS v. Stevic*, 467 U.S. 407 (1984). The operative language of section 101(a)(42)(A) of the Act is as follows:

> The term "refugee" means (A) any person who is outside any country of such person's nationality or, in the case of a person having no nationality, is outside any country in which such person last habitually resided, and who is unable or unwilling to return to, and is unable or unwilling to avail himself or herself of the protection of that country because of persecution or a well-founded fear of persecution on account of race, religion, nationality, membership in a particular social group, or political opinion, . . .

An applicant can establish *persecution* by showing that he or she has been punished or harmed for one or more of the five statutory grounds in the definition of refugee quoted above. *See* 8 C.F.R. § 1208.13(b)(1).

An applicant can establish a *well-founded fear of persecution* by showing that a reasonable person would fear future persecution upon return to his or her native country or country of residence. *Matter of Mogharrabi*, 19 I&N Dec. 439, at 445 (BIA 1987).

A reasonable fear of persecution is not only a subjective fear. In addition, an applicant must establish that:

1) the applicant possesses a belief or characteristic connected to one of the 5 statutory grounds in the definition of refugee;
2) the applicant has been targeted for punishment or harm based on that belief or characteristic or falls within a group subjected to a pattern or practice of punishment or harm based on that belief or characteristic;
3) the persecutor is aware or could become aware that the applicant possesses that belief or characteristic or is a member of a group defined by that belief or characteristic;
4) the persecutor has the capability to punish or harm the applicant;
5) the persecutor has the inclination to punish or harm the applicant; and
6) internal relocation to avoid the risk of persecution is not reasonable.

See Matter of Acosta, 19 I&N Dec. 211 (BIA 1985), as modified by *Matter of Mogharrabi*, *supra.*; *See* 8 C.F.R. § 1208.13(b)(2).

Country of Nationality or Last Habitual Residence

The first nuance in the definition of refugee that is sometimes overlooked is that the asylum applicant must establish persecution or the risk of persecution in the country of his or her nationality, not just any country. Only persons who have no nationality can frame an asylum claim by establishing persecution or the risk of persecution in the last country of habitual residence. An example of this is a stateless person such as a Palestinian who is living outside of the Palestinian territories. The Third Circuit Court of Appeals struggled with the definition of "last country of habitual residence" in *Paripovic v. Gonzales*, 418 F.3d 240 (3rd Cir. 2005). Ultimately, the Third Circuit Court of Appeals rejected the notion of intent and/or choice as a way of defining habitual residence and affirmed reliance on duration of time to conclude that 2 years of residence was sufficient to establish habitual residence for a stateless person. *Paripovic v. Gonzales*, at 245.

Issues relating to nationality, stateless persons and habitual residence can also arise when an asylum applicant asserts persecution or the risk of persecution in a country where he or she is residing that is not the country of the asylum applicant's nationality. For example, a national of Albania who has been given permanent resident status in Germany (the asylum applicant's last country of habitual residence) cannot frame an asylum claim based on persecution or the risk of persecution in Germany if he or she is not a German national. As a national of Albania, the asylum applicant in this hypothetical must establish persecution or a risk of persecution in Albania. Obviously, the definition of nationality can become a threshold issue in an asylum claim. The definition of nationality for purposes of immigration proceedings is as follows: "The term 'national' means a person owing permanent allegiance to a state." *See* section 101(a)(21) of the Act. Application of foreign law regarding nationality might become a controlling factor in a case involving an asylum applicant who is not stateless and attempts to establish persecution or a risk of persecution in a country other than the country where he or she is a national.

Level of Harm

An asylum applicant must establish a level of punishment or harm that is sufficient to classify as persecution. The punishment or harm alleged in an asylum application must be extreme enough or egregious enough to classify as persecution. Persecution in the context of asylum law does not include every type of abuse that our society perceives as offensive or unlawful. *See Arif v. Mukasey*, 509 F.3d 677, 680 (5th Cir. 2007); *Fatin v. INS*, 12 F.3d 1233, 1243 (3rd Cir. 1993); *Korablina v. INS*, 158 F.3d 1038, 1034 (9th Cir. 1998). For this reason, mere threats, harassment, intimidation, interrogations, discrimination, etc. without more will not ordinarily be enough to establish persecution. Even physical violence in the form of beatings causing bruising and bleeding and brief periods of incarceration are not usually considered to be punishment or harm that is overwhelming enough to classify as persecution. The asylum applicant, therefore, must be prepared to provide evidence in sufficient detail about the severity of past abuse or the anticipated abuse if returned to the applicant's country of nationality or last habitual residence. For example, if an asylum applicant has been psychologically traumatized by punishment or harm it would be wise to obtain a psychological evaluation to determine if he or she is suffering from post traumatic stress. The details of the punishment or harm are important. For example, the Seventh Circuit Court of Appeals determined that a single incident of abuse can constitute persecution as long as the specifics reveal the severity of the situation. *Irasoc v. Mukasey*, 522 F.3d 727 (7th Cir. 2008). In the *Irasoc* case there was not only evidence of hand cuffing and loss of consciousness. The record reflected that extreme pain levels caused by repeated beatings and forcibly kicking Irasoc's testicles led to unconsciousness. Representation of asylum applicants is not for the squeamish or faint of heart.

Do not ask the Immigration Judge to examine marks or damaged body parts during the asylum hearing. Not only is the Immigration Judge as well the attorneys present not competent to examine a person's body and interpret whatever is revealed, but a picture is worth a thousand words for review on appeal. Here's a courtroom exchange that demonstrates what not to do in an immigration hearing:

Q: What – did they beat you with anything other than their hands. . .?

APPROACHING THE BENCH FROM INSIDE THE IMMIGRATION COURT

A: They. . .and I have a big mark on my butt and I could show it to you.

JUDGE TO _____ (Attorney)

A: Would Your Honor wish to see it? It's on her hip and not on her butt.

Q: Well, no. I'm not a physician. I'm not in any position to evaluate marks on someone's body.

A: We're not asking that. We're asking to acknowledge whether, in fact, she has a mark on her body.

Q: That's not something I'm going to do at a hearing. If you wanted to do that properly, you could have had photographs, had some kind of testimony with regard to the photograph. I'm not going to conduct physical examinations in the courtroom.

A: Okay, Your Honor. I guess the fact of the matter is that –

Q: She's testified that it's here. We're just going to have to rely on her testimony. I don't have any reason to doubt her at this point.

A: We weren't able to find any physicians who could do it free and there were none available so –

Q: You have a camera.

A: Your Honor would take a photograph of her scar –

Q: Sure.

A: -- without expert testimony?

Q: Accompanied with testimony if someone who was there when it was taken can verify that it was taken of her.

A: Okay. She could show it to you.

Q: It's not that complicated.

A: All right.

[Portions of the above excerpt have been redacted to protect the identity of the respondent.]

If you have a picture a written evaluation by a medical specialist should accompany the picture. Even a Supreme Court Justice is not medically competent to evaluate and interpret scars, marks and mutilated or missing body parts. If you can't afford or find a medical specialist to evaluate or explain the pictured evidence the strength of the evidence diminishes to the extent that various uninformed conclusions might be drawn, but at least the record will contain evidence that might corroborate the respondent's testimony and conclusions.

Nexus With Protected Grounds

Many unsuccessful asylum applications fail because the applicant cannot establish a connection between the motive of the alleged persecutor and one of the 5 statutory grounds in the definition of refugee. It is not enough to establish egregious punishment or harm or a risk of egregious punishment or harm that should be classified as persecution. For example, there might be a risk of death or severe punishment or harm if an alien is removed from the United States. However, if that risk of death or severe punishment or harm is not motivated by race, religion, nationality, membership in a particular social group or political opinion the alien is not eligible for asylum in the United States.

In my experience, persecution based on race is not as commonly alleged as a basis for an asylum claim as some might expect. Persecution based on religion seems to be more common. An example of a religious persecution claim arises among Chinese nationals who sometimes allege persecution for membership in an unregistered church. According to these asylum applicants, the Chinese government controls the practice of religion in China by requiring churches to register with the government and insists on appointing or otherwise manipulating the leaders of the registered churches. These applicants often describe arrests, detentions, interrogations and physical abuse, as well formal sentencing for participation in unregistered church activities in China. Other countries where religious based asylum claims are not unusual are India, Pakistan, Indonesia, Nigeria and generally the Middle East.

Nationality is sometimes alleged as a motivation for persecution in countries like Ethiopia that have experienced territorial division following civil war. For example, Eritrea, once part of Ethiopia, became independent at the end of fighting approximately in December 2000. Many human rights abuses sometimes based on imputed Ethiopian or Eritrean nationality or allegiances have persisted after active fighting ceased.

Membership in a particular social group is at the same time one of the most common grounds for persecution alleged in asylum applications and the most nebulous. The BIA has established a standard for identifying a particular social group as follows:

> The members of a particular social group must share a common, immutable characteristic, which may be an innate one, such as sex, color, or kinship ties, or a shared past experience, such as former military leadership or land ownership, but it must be one that the members of the group either cannot change, or should not be required to change,

because it is fundamental to their individual identities or consciences.

Matter of Acosta, 19 I&N Dec. 211 (BIA 1985); *followed in Matter of C-A-*, 23 I&N Dec. 951 (BIA 2006). The BIA has also required social visibility as an essential property of a particular social group. The particular social group's shared characteristic must make the group readily identifiable in society and the group must be defined with sufficient particularity to limit membership. *Matter of A-M-E- & J-G-U-*, 24 I&N Dec. 69 (BIA 2007).

Asylum seekers sometimes make the mistake of defining a particular social group by the type of punishment or harm the group experiences. For example, an asylum applicant may be able to credibly establish membership in a group defined by any number of immutable characteristics (e.g. sex, color, kinship ties, or a shared past experience fundamental to individual identity) that is at risk of some specific kind of punishment or harm in the country of his or her nationality or last country of habitual residence. This, without more, does not establish a risk of persecution that will support an asylum claim. The asylum applicant must take one more step to prove that the risk of punishment or harm is on account of the group's immutable characteristics. *See for example Matter of Sanchez and Escobar*, 19 I&N Dec. 276 (BIA 1985) (". . .it is not enough to simply identify the common characteristics of a statistical grouping of a portion of the population at risk, but. . .there must be a showing that the claimed persecution is on account of the group's identifying characteristics."); *Rreshpja v. Gonzales*, 420 F.3d 551, 555-56 (6th Cir. 2005) (stating that "a social group may not be circularly defined by the fact that it suffers persecution").

Political opinion is a commonly alleged ground in asylum claims. It is important to distinguish between the agenda or goals of the persecutor and the specific motive for punishing or harming the asylum applicant. The agenda and goals of the persecutor do not usually govern the outcome of a persecution claim, but the specific

Excuses For Criminal Behavior

"I shouldn't be deported. I should get asylum because the man I killed was in the opposition party, and the fight was caused by a political argument."

Generally, an applicant for asylum cannot establish persecution even though other persons have been harmed or killed. *See, for example, Nyonzele v. INS*, 83 F.3d 975, 983 (8th Cir.1996) (isolated acts of violence to those other than the asylum applicant insufficient to establish persecution). Another twist in the circumstances underlying the excuse described above is that the killing took place in the United States and the author of the excuse was convicted for murder.

motive for punishing or harming the asylum applicant is crucial and must be linked to at least one of the 5 grounds in the definition of refugee that characterizes the asylum applicant. The United States Supreme Court clarified the distinction between persecutor agenda and specific motive for persecution in *INS v. Zacarias*, 570 U.S. 478 (1992). In the *Zacarias* decision, the United States Supreme Court determined that a guerrilla organization's attempt to force Zacarias into military service did not, without more, establish persecution based on Zacarias' political opinion, even though Zacarias was politically opposed to the guerrillas. According to *INS v. Zacarias*, a victim of coercive recruitment must establish that the victim has been targeted because of the victim's political opinion, and that the persecution is not solely the consequence of the guerrillas' agenda to increase their ranks to carry out a war with the government or pursue their political goal, the guerrillas' political goal being irrelevant. In other words, an asylum applicant claiming persecution on account of political opinion must tie punishment or harm to the asylum applicant's political opinion, rather than establish that asylum applicant was a victim of the persecutor's pursuit of the persecutor's political agenda. If the asylum applicant only establishes opposition to the political goals of the persecutor, without more, he or she has not established eligibility for asylum.

It should be noted with regard to claims based on political opinion that, according to the definition of refugee, a person who:

1) has been forced to abort a pregnancy;
2) has been forced to undergo involuntary sterilization;
3) has been persecuted for failure or refusal to abort a pregnancy or undergo involuntary sterilization; or
4) has been persecuted for resistance to a coercive population control program

shall be deemed to have been persecuted on account of political opinion. Also, a person who has a well-founded fear of any of the above described circumstances in the future shall be deemed to have a well-founded fear of persecution on account of political opinion. *See* section 101(a)(42)(B) of the Act.

Discretion

Based on the definition of refugee, establishing past persecution *or* a well-founded fear of persecution qualifies an alien as a refugee and at the same time establishes eligibility for asylum. However, once an applicant establishes eligibility for asylum, the asylum application may or may not be granted in the exercise of discretion. *Matter of Pula*, 19 I&N Dec. 467, 473-74 (BIA 1987); *See* § 1208.14(a). The BIA in *Matter of Pula* used a totality of circumstances approach to the exercise of discretion and identified the following factors:

1) whether orderly refugee procedures were available to the applicant in an country through which he or she passed and whether the applicant made any attempt to seek asylum before coming to the United States;

2) the length of time an applicant remained in a third country, and his living conditions, safety, and potential for long term residence;

3) whether the applicant's personal ties to the United States may have caused the applicant to seek asylum in the United States rather than elsewhere, and whether the applicant has personal ties in another country where he does not fear persecution;

4) the seriousness of fraud on the part of the applicant, if any; and

5) general humanitarian considerations such as the applicant's health and age.

In *Matter of Pula*, the BIA indicated that a real danger of persecution should ordinarily outweigh all but the most egregious adverse factors.

An asylum applicant who establishes past persecution is presumed to have a well-founded fear of future persecution. *See* 8 C.F.R. § 1208.13(b)(1)(i). However, an application for asylum must be denied in the exercise of discretion if the DHS establishes that a well-founded fear of future persecution does not actually exist. The only way for an asylum applicant to avoid denial in these circumstances is to demonstrate compelling reasons for being unwilling to return to the applicant's country of nationality or last country of habitual residence arising out of the severity of the past persecution or the reasonable possibility of other serious harm upon removal to that country. *Matter of N-M-A-*, 22 I&N Dec. 312 (BIA 1998). *See* 8 C.F.R. § 1208.15. This is often labeled "humanitarian asylum," but in reality all asylum grants are based on humanitarian grounds. Nevertheless, establishing past persecution is a giant step toward an asylum grant in most cases.

Mandatory Denial

Governing law and regulations dictate mandatory denial of asylum applications in certain specific circumstances. The circumstances requiring mandatory denial are as follows:

1) the alien ordered, incited, assisted, or otherwise participated in the persecution of any person on account of race, religion nationality, membership in a particular social group, or political opinion;

2) the alien, having been convicted by a final judgment of a particularly serious crime, constitutes a danger to the community of the United States;

3) there are serious reasons for believing that the alien has committed a serious nonpolitical crime outside the United States;

4) there are reasonable grounds for regarding the alien as a danger to the security of the United States;

5) the alien has engaged in terrorist activity; or
6) the alien was firmly resettled in another country prior to arriving in the United States.

See section 208(b)(2)(A) of the Act. Mandatory denial of asylum applications involving persecution of others and terrorism activities does not seem to be as common as the other grounds for mandatory denial. Therefore, no further commentary will be made with regard to them. However, terrorist activities as described in sections 212(a)(3)(B)(i) and 237(a)(4)(B) of the Act are broadly defined and nebulous. Sometimes, the DHS will assert that a respondent is a persecutor or has engaged in terrorist activities based on mere service in the military of a country where there is reason to believe that certain military units have committed serious human rights abuses. That alone should not be enough to establish that the asylum applicant is a persecutor or has engaged in terrorist activities, but it will significantly complicate and lengthen the asylum hearing.

As noted above, asylum must be denied if the asylum applicant, having been convicted by final judgment of a particularly serious crime in the United States constitutes a danger to the community. *See* 8 C.F.R. § 1208.13(c). To determine whether an alien has been convicted for a particularly serious crime, it is necessary to consider:

1) the nature of the conviction;
2) the type of sentence imposed;
3) the circumstances and underlying facts of the conviction; and
4) whether the circumstances and underlying facts indicate a danger to the community.

Matter of Frentescu, 18 I&N Dec. 244 (BIA 1982); *Matter of S-S-*, 22 I&N Dec. 458 (BIA 1999); *Matter of N-A-M-*, 24 I&N Dec. 336 (BIA 2007).

Once a finding is made that an alien has been finally convicted for a particularly serious crime, it necessarily follows that the alien is a danger to the community of the United States. It is not necessary for the Immigration Judge to make any additional finding with regard to the likelihood of future serious misconduct on the part of the alien. *Matter of Carballe*, 19 I&N Dec. 357 (BIA 1986*); Matter of B-*, 20 I&N Dec. 427, 430 (BIA 1991).

There is a special rule for classifying aggravated felonies (defined under section 101(a)(43) of the Act) as particularly serious crimes. *See* section 208(b)(2)(B)(i) of the Act. In short, any aggravated felony conviction is a conviction for a particularly serious crime and requires mandatory denial of the convicted alien's asylum application. *Matter of K-*, 20 I&N Dec. 418 (BIA 1991); *Matter of C-*, 20 I&N Dec. 529 (BIA 1992).

Where there are serious reasons for believing that an alien has committed a serious nonpolitical crime outside the United States before arrival in the United States, the alien is not eligible for asylum. *See* section 208(b)(2)(A)(iii) of the Act. The BIA has determined that a "serious crime" must be a capital crime or a very grave punishable act and not a minor offense punishable by moderate sentences. *Matter of Rodriguez-Palma*, 17 I&N Dec. 465 (BIA 1980). It is important to note that *Matter of Rodriguez-Palma* has been modified on other grounds by subsequent decision. *See Matter of Gonzalez*, 19 I&N Dec. 682 (BIA 1988).

Asylum must be denied if the applicant is firmly resettled outside the United States. *See* section 208(b)(2)(A)(vi). An alien is considered to be firmly resettled if, prior to arrival in the United States, another nation has offered the alien permanent resident status, citizenship, or some other type of permanent resettlement, unless the alien establishes:

1) that the alien's entry into that nation was a necessary consequence of flight from persecution, that the alien stayed in that nation only as long as necessary to arrange onward

travel, and that the alien did not establish significant ties with that nation; or

2) that conditions of residence in that nation were so substantially and consciously restricted by governmental authority that the alien was not in fact resettled.

See 8 C.F.R. § 1208.15.

Specific factors that must be considered when determining whether conditions of residence were too restricted to establish firm resettlement are:

1) conditions under which other residents of the country live;
2) whether temporary or permanent housing was made available;
3) the types and extent of employment available;
4) the extent to which the alien was permitted to own property; and
5) other privileges such as travel rights, education, public aid, and naturalization.

See 8 C.F.R. § 1208.15(b). *See Matter of D-X- & Y-Z-*, 25 I&N Dec. 664 (BIA 2012). The DHS, however, has the initial burden of proof to make a *prima facie* showing (i.e. legalese meaning "superficial" showing) of an offer of firm resettlement by presenting evidence that the alien can stay indefinitely in a country outside the United States. *Matter of A-G-G-*, 25 I&N Dec. 486 (BIA 2011).

Withholding of Removal

Withholding of removal under section 241(b)(3) of the Act is mandatory rather than discretionary. To qualify for withholding of removal, an applicant must establish a clear probability of persecution which means that persecution is "more likely than not." *INS v. Cardoza-Fonseca*, 480 U.S. 421 (1987). *See* 8 C.F.R. § 1208.16. The key differences between withholding of removal and asylum are the mandatory nature of withholding of removal and a heightened burden of persuasion. If the applicant establishes persecution or the risk of persecution in his or her country of nationality or last country of habitual residence is "more likely than not" (as opposed to a preponderance of evidence standard for asylum applications) the Immigration Judge must grant the withholding of removal application, unless the application is subject to mandatory denial. The same grounds for mandatory denial that apply to asylum applications apply to withholding of removal applications, except firm resettlement. *See* section 241(b)(3)(B) of the Act; 8 C.F.R. § 1208.16(c)(2). Governing statutes and regulations do not require denial of an application for withholding of removal if an alien has been found to be firmly resettled. Therefore, denial of an alien's asylum application based on firm resettlement does not require denial of withholding of removal as well. *See Matter of Soleimani*, 20 I&N Dec. 99, at 100, n.2 (BIA 1989). Compare section 208(b)(2)(A) of the Act with section 241(b)(3)(B) of the Act. However, special conditions relating to classification of an aggravated felony as a particularly serious crime that require mandatory denial are different for withholding of removal applications. As noted above in the discussion of asylum, any conviction for an aggravated felony requires mandatory denial of the asylum application. However, for withholding of removal applications, a conviction for an aggravated felony is a particularly serious crime on its face only if a sentence of 5 years or more has been assessed as punishment. If a withholding of removal applicant has been convicted of multiple aggravated felonies one or more of the aggravated felony convictions will be classified as a crime or crimes that are particularly serious on the face of the record only if all the sentences added together (i.e. aggregate sentences) amount to 5 years or more. *See* section 241(b)(3)(B) of the Act; 8 C.F.R. § 1208.16(d)(2), (3). Regardless of the 5 year sentence requirement for automatic classification of aggravated felonies as particularly serious crimes, an aggravated felony can nevertheless be classified as a particularly serious crime on a case by case basis using the same criteria discussed above with regard to asylum applications. See section 241(b)(3)(B) of the Act; 8 C.F.R. § 1208.16(d)(2), (3).

Since the sentence assessed as punishment for an aggravated felony sometimes governs classification of the aggravated felony as a particularly serious crime in the context of a withholding of removal hearing, it is important to realize that actual incarceration is not required for the sentence to be used for the purpose of classifying the aggravated felony as a particularly serious crime. Under section 101(a)(48)(B) of the Act;

> Any reference to a term of imprisonment with respect to an offense is deemed to include the period of incarceration or confinement ordered by a court of law regardless of any suspension of the imposition or execution of that imprisonment or sentence in whole or in part.

Section 101(a)(48)(B) of the Act applies to convictions and sentences entered before, on, or after September 30, 1996 (i.e. applicable retroactively). *See* section 322(c) of the IIRIRA. *Matter of S-S-*, 21 I&N Dec. 900 (BIA 1997).

Attorneys who successfully obtain a grant of withholding of removal for a client should not be surprised when the Immigration Judge also orders the client removed to a country other than the country where the risk of persecution exists. A grant of withholding of removal is country specific and the DHS can remove an alien who has been granted withholding of removal by following the prioritized approach found in section 241(b)(1) of the Act. *See* 8 C.F.R. §§ 241.15 and 241.25. It might calm the nerves of some to know that during the 35 years that I have worked for the federal government I have never heard of an actual removal to a third country after a grant of withholding of removal. It appears that the main reason aliens granted withholding of removal are rarely removed to a third country is the inability of the United States government to find another country that will accept such aliens. Finally, unlike aliens who have been granted asylum, an alien who has been granted withholding of removal has no prospects of adjustment to permanent resident status directly arising from the grant of withholding of removal.

Burden of Proof

Even lawyers can become confused about the distinction between burden of proof and burden of persuasion. In simple terms, the burden of proof describes the statutory elements that must be proven for a specific purpose, such as the elements required to establish a removal charge or the criteria required to establish eligibility for relief from removal. The burden of persuasion relates to the evidence introduced into the record to carry the burden of proof. Therefore, depending on the reliability or trustworthiness and quantity of evidence submitted by the litigants, the burden of persuasion may shift from one litigant to the other in the course of court proceedings. The burden of proof, however, always remains with the party to whom it is assigned by law. The burden of proof is a matter of law. The burden of persuasion is a matter of fact.

The general rule in immigration proceedings is that the party charged with the burden of proof must carry the burden of proof by a preponderance of the evidence. *Matter of Acosta*, 19 I&N Dec. 211, at 215-16 (BIA 1985). *See* 8 C.F.R. § 1240.8(d).

Congress amended section 208(b)(1) of the Act to provide guidance relating to the asylum applicant's burden of proof and persuasion. *See* section 101(a)(3) of the REAL ID Act of 2005; Pub. L. No. 109-13, Div. B, 119 Stat. 231 (2005). *See* section 208(b)(1)(B) of the Act. Under section 101(h) of the REAL ID Act, the amendments relating to the asylum applicant's burden of proof take effect on or before the date of enactment which is May 11, 2005. Therefore, these amendments apply to applications for asylum filed on or after May 11, 2005. Furthermore, the BIA has held that the same amendments relating to the burden of proof for asylum applicants also govern applications for withholding of removal. *Matter of C-T-L-*, 25 I&N Dec. 341 (BIA 2010). Specifically, the REAL ID Act amendments, codified at section 208(b)(1)(B)(i) of the Act, require that an asylum applicant or withholding of removal applicant must establish that race, religion, nationality, membership in a particular social group, or political opinion was or will be at least one *central reason* for persecuting the applicant. The REAL ID Act amendments give Immigration Judges broad discretionary authority to require corroborating evidence, unless the applicant does not have the evidence and cannot reasonably obtain it. The REAL ID Act also authorizes Immigration Judges to consider the totality of circumstances and all relevant factors, for the purpose of making credibility determinations. Some of the factors identified in the REAL ID Act as grounds for making credibility determinations are: demeanor; candor or responsiveness of an applicant or witness; the inherent plausibility of the applicant's or witness' account; consistency between oral and written accounts; internal consistency of statements; the consistency of statements in the context of other evidence; inaccuracies or falsehoods in statements (regardless of whether or not such inconsistencies, inaccuracies or falsehoods go to the heart of an applicant's claim); and any other relevant factor. *See* section 208(b)(1)(B)(i) of the Act.

Convention Against Torture

The United States signed the United Nations Convention Against Torture and other Forms of Cruel, Inhuman or Degrading Treatment or Punishment (the "Convention Against Torture") treaty on October 18, 1988. The United States Senate ratified the treaty on October 27, 1990, and the Convention Against Torture became binding on the United States on November 20, 1994. *See* 136 Cong. Rec. S17,486, S17,492 (daily ed. Oct. 27, 1990) and 74 Interpreter Releases, No. 45, Nov. 21, 1997, at 1773, 1781 (citing U.N. Doc. No. 571 Leg/SER. E/13, IV.9 (1992). The Convention Against Torture was not implemented until enactment of section 2242 of the Foreign Affairs Reform and Restructuring Act of 1998 (Pub. Law 105-277, Div. G, Oct. 21, 1998) which required implementation no later than 120 days after enactment (March 22, 1999). Before implementation, Immigration Judges lacked jurisdiction to adjudicate Convention Against Torture claims. *Matter of H-M-V-*, 21 I&N Dec. 3365 (BIA 1998).

An applicant for relief under Article 3 of the Convention Against Torture must apply for withholding of removal under 8 C.F.R. § 1208.16(c) (not to be confused with withholding of removal under section 241(b)(3) of the Act). To qualify for relief under the Convention Against Torture, an applicant must prove that torture would be *more likely than not* for the applicant if he or she is removed to the proposed country of removal.

Unlike asylum applicants and withholding of removal applicants under sections 208 and 241(b)(3) of the Act, an applicant for withholding of removal under the Convention Against Torture is not required to establish refugee status by proving persecution arising from race, religion, nationality, membership in a particular social group, or political opinion. However, there are independent criteria for Convention Against Torture applications.

For the purpose of determining eligibility for relief for withholding of removal under the Convention Against Torture, "torture" means the intentional infliction of severe mental or physical pain or suffering, for an illicit purpose, at the instigation or with the consent or acquiescence of a public official or other person acting in an official capacity while the targeted person is in the custody or physical control of the perpetrator. *See* 8 C.F.R. § 1208.18(a)(1), (6). To qualify as torture, mental pain or suffering must be prolonged harm arising from: 1) intentional infliction or threatened infliction of severe physical pain or suffering; 2) administration or threatened administration of mind altering substances or procedures intended to profoundly disrupt the senses or personality; or 3) a threat of imminent death to the applicant or another. *See* 8 C.F.R. § 1208.18(a)(4). Unanticipated severity of pain or suffering does not constitute torture. *See* 8 C.F.R. § 1208.18(a)(5). Torture also does not include lesser forms of cruel, inhuman treatment, or degrading treatment, such as the infliction of pain or suffering arising only from lawful sanctions. *Matter of J-E-*, 23 I&N Dec. 291 (BIA 2002).

Acquiescence of a public official requires awareness of torture activity and a breach of legal responsibility to intervene. *See* 8 C.F.R. § 1208.18(a)(7). A majority of the circuit courts of appeal appear to have adopted a "willful blindness" test to determine whether a government acquiesces to acts of torture. *See Zheng v. Ashcroft*, 332 F.3d 1186 (9th Cir. 2003); *Khouzam v. Ashcroft*, 361 F.3d 161 (2nd Cir. 2004); *Cruz-Funez v. Gonzales*, 406 F.3d 1187 (10th Cir. 2005); *Hakim v. Holder*, 638 F.3d 151 (5th Cir. 2010). The "willful blindness" test should be contrasted to the "willful acceptance" test applied by the BIA in *Matter of S-V-*, 22 I&N Dec. 1306 (BIA 2000) and by the Attorney General in *Matter of Y-L-, A-G- & R-S-R*, 23 I&N Dec. 270 (A.G. 2003). *See also Kasneci v. Gonzales*, 415 F.3d 202, 205 (1st Cir. 2005) (consent and acquiescence of a public official necessary for protection under the Convention Against Torture). Willful acceptance requires deliberate acceptance of torture (i.e. awareness and approval of torture). Willful blindness, on the other hand, only requires awareness of torture and taking no action to intervene (i.e. awareness and omission to act).

Examples of illicit purposes are:

1) obtaining information or confession;
2) extrajudicial punishment;
3) intimidation or coercion; or
4) discrimination.

See 8 C.F.R. § 1208.18(a)(1). *Matter of J-E-, supra.* These examples are not exclusive.

To determine whether an applicant would be tortured, all relevant evidence including, but not limited to the following, must be considered:

1) evidence of past torture;
2) evidence of flagrant human rights violations within the proposed country of removal;
3) relevant information about other conditions in the proposed country of removal; and
4) evidence that the applicant could relocate within the proposed country of removal to avoid the likelihood of torture.

See 8 C.F.R. § 1208.16(c)(3).

Withholding of removal under the Convention Against Torture is mandatory; not discretionary. The applicant is entitled to relief upon establishing eligibility. *See* 8 C.F.R. § 1208.16(c)(4). However, governing regulations impose specific conditions for mandatory denial which are the same as the conditions for mandatory denial of withholding of removal applications under section 241(b)(3) of the Act. *See* 8 C.F.R. § 1208.16(d)(2) and section 241(b)(3)(B) of the Act.

Deferral of Removal

Unlike applicants for withholding of removal under section 241(b)(3) of the Act, if an eligible applicant for withholding of removal under the Convention Against Torture is subject to mandatory denial the applicant must be granted deferral of removal under 8 C.F.R. § 1208.17(a). A beneficiary of deferral of removal does not gain legal status in the United States. An Immigration Judge must instruct an alien granted deferral of removal that:

1) deferral of the applicant's removal will be effective only until terminated;
2) removal to the proposed country of removal will be temporarily deferred until it is determined that torture of the applicant would be unlikely;
3) deferral of the applicant's removal does not give any lawful permanent resident status to the applicant;

APPROACHING THE BENCH FROM INSIDE THE IMMIGRATION COURT

4) the DHS may remove the applicant to another country (other than the proposed country of removal where the likelihood of torture exists) that is willing to accept the applicant; and

5) if in custody a grant of deferral of the applicant's removal does not mean the applicant will be released.

See 8 C.F.R. § 1208.17(b).

Chapter IV

Hardship Claims

Cancellation of Removal For Nonpermanent Residents

§ection 240A(b)(1) of the Act provides that the Attorney General may cancel the removal from the United States of an alien who is inadmissible or deportable if certain criteria are met. To be eligible for this form of relief, and applicant must prove that:

1) the applicant has been continuously physically present in the United States for at least 10 years immediately preceding the application date;
2) the applicant has been a person of good moral character for 10 years;
3) the applicant has not been convicted for an offense classified under sections 212(a)(2), 237(a)(2), or 237(a)(3) of the Act (criminals or document fraud); and
4) the applicant's removal from the United States would result in *exceptional and extremely unusual hardship* to the applicant's United States citizen or lawful permanent resident spouse, parent, or child.

A removable alien who has been battered or subjected to extreme cruelty in the United States by a United States citizen or lawful permanent resident spouse or parent, or an alien who is the parent of a child who has been battered or subjected to extreme cruelty by the child's United States citizen or lawful permanent resident parent may apply for cancellation of removal under a more relaxed standard. *See* section 240A(b)(2) of the Act. To be eligible for relief under this relaxed standard, the applicant must prove that:

1) the applicant has been continuously physically present in the United States for at least 3 years immediately preceding the application date;

2) the applicant has been a person of good moral character during the same 3 year period;

3) the applicant is not inadmissible under sections 212(a)(2) or (3) of the Act (criminals or document fraud) and is not deportable under sections 237(a)(1)(G), (2), (3), or (4) of the Act (marriage fraud, criminals, document fraud, or security related grounds);

4) the applicant has not been convicted for an aggravated felony defined under section 101(a)(43) of the Act; and

5) the applicant's removal from the United States would result in *extreme hardship* to the applicant, the applicant's child, or (if the applicant is a child) the applicant's parent.

Once the applicant has established eligibility for cancellation of removal, the application may be granted or denied in the exercise of discretion.

Each threshold criterion for cancellation of removal has been the subject of litigation. So it might be helpful to address each one.

Physical Presence

Section 240A(d) of the Act provides that continuous physical presence ends under the following circumstances:

1) when the applicant is served with an NTA (form I-862) or an Order to Show Cause ("OSC," Form I-221) (utilized to initiate deportation proceedings before the effective date

APPROACHING THE BENCH FROM INSIDE THE IMMIGRATION COURT

of IIRIRA) according to *Matter of Nolasco*, 22 I&N Dec. 632 (BIA 1999);

2) when the applicant commits a crime that renders the applicant inadmissible under section 212(a)(2) of the Act or removable under sections 237(a)(2) and/or 237(a)(4) of the Act (criminals and/or security or security related grounds);

3) if the alien has departed from the United States for more than 90 days or an aggregate period exceeding 180 days.

Continuous presence is not required if the applicant:

1) has served at least 24 months in active duty status in the armed forces of the United States and has been honorably discharged from such service; and

2) at the time of induction or enlistment, the applicant was in the United States.

Since the date of service of the NTA cuts off physical presence, the easiest way to calculate whether an applicant for cancellation of removal can establish the required 10 years of continuous physical presence is to subtract the date of arrival from the date of service of the NTA or OSC. If the difference is less than 10 years the cancellation of removal application must be denied as a matter of law.

Under section 309(c)(5) of IIRIRA, the above described continuous physical presence provisions take effect "before, on, or after" September 30, 1996 (the IIRIRA date of enactment).

The BIA has determined that the specific list of circumstances that cut off physical presence in section 240A(d) of the Act is not exclusive. *Matter of Romalez*, 23 I&N Dec. 423, 429 (BIA 2002). For example, if an alien is given a voluntary return pursuant to 240B(b)(1) of the Act or is refused admission after being afforded a formal documented procedure under threat of being placed in immigration court proceedings the alien's return to a country outside the United States is deemed to cut off continuous physical presence, even though this circumstance is not listed under section 240A(d) of the Act. *Matter of Avilez-Nava*, 23 I&N Dec. 799 (BIA 2005). *See McClovin v. INS*, 648 F.2d 935 (4ᵗʰ Cir. 1981). Other activities connected with departure that have resulted in the cut-off of continuous physical presence are alien smuggling and sham marriage. *See Matter of Contreras*, 18 I&N Dec. 30 (BIA 1981) and *Matter of Herrera*, 18 I&N Dec. 4 (BIA 1981), respectively.

Good Moral Character

Unlike the calculation of the 10 year time period required for continuous physical presence, the 10 year time period for good moral character is calculated by counting backward from the date on which the application is finally resolved by the Immigration Judge or the BIA. *Matter of Ortega-Cabrera*, 23 I&N Dec. 793 (BIA 2005). In other words, the 10 year time period for good moral character continues to progress until a final administrative decision is made. Imagine a train pulling 10 cars along a track until reaching a final destination. Only the portion of the track occupied by the 10 cars is subject to consideration.

Good moral character is defined negatively under section 101(f) of the Act. No person can be found to be a person of good moral character who is or has been:

1) a habitual drunkard (section 101(f)(1) of the Act);
2) classifiable as a prostitute or person involved in prostitution or other commercialized vice, a person who has been convicted of a crime involving moral turpitude or has admitted the elements of such crime, a person who has been convicted of 2 or more crimes for which the aggregate sentences imposed were 5 years or more, an alien smuggler, polygamist, a person convicted for a narcotics offense or a person who has admitted committing the elements of such offense (committed during the period under review), or a drug trafficker (section 101(f)(3) of the Act);

Excuses For Criminal Behavior

Q: You were arrested for Driving While Intoxicated in 2008. How did that happen?

A: I was drinking at home, and drove to the store to get some beer. While I was driving to the store, I noticed a police car in the next lane and my car went into the same lane as the police car. That got the attention of the police officer.

Driving while intoxicated is not considered to be a crime involving moral turpitude because the state is not required to prove intent of any kind. "[I]t is in the intent that moral turpitude inheres." *United States ex rel. Meyer v. Day*, 54 F.2d 336, 337 (2d Cir. 1931).

3) a person whose income is derived principally from illegal gambling (section 101(f)(4) of the Act);
4) a person who has been convicted of 2 or more gambling offenses during the period under review (section 101(f)(5) of the Act);
5) a person who has given false testimony to obtain immigration benefits (section 101(f)(6) of the Act);
6) a person who has been confined for a criminal conviction for 180 days or more during the period under review (section 101(f)(7) of the Act);
7) a person who has been convicted of an aggravated felony at any time (section 101(f)(8) of the Act); or
8) a person who at any time has engaged in conduct described under section 212(a)(3)(c) of the Act (relating to assistance in Nazi persecution, participation in genocide or commission of acts of torture or extrajudicial killings) or 212(a)(2)(G) of the Act (relating to severe violations of religious freedom) (section 101(f)(9) of the Act).

The list described above is not exclusive. Thus, a person who is not specifically described in the list may be found not to be a person of good moral character for other reasons.

Classification of an applicant's offense as a crime involving moral turpitude will not only disqualify the applicant for cancellation of removal based on failure to establish good moral character during the time period under review. Conviction for an offense involving moral turpitude also disqualifies an applicant for cancellation of removal as an offense described under sections 212(a)(2) or 237(a)(2) of the Act, regardless of whether or not the offense is committed within the time period under review. *See Matter of Almanza*, 24 I&N Dec. 771 (BIA 2009); *Matter of Cortez*, 25 I&N Dec. 301 (BIA 2010); *Matter of Pedroza*, 25 I&N Dec. 312 (BIA 2010).

It appears that the BIA might have committed error by recognizing the petty offense exception as an exemption from cancellation of removal disqualification for respondents convicted of a crime involving moral turpitude, who are not battered spouses or children. The *Almanza* decision does not address the difference between the disqualifying language found at section 240A(b)(1)(C) of the Act and the disqualifying language found at section 240A(b)(2)(A)(iv) of the Act. The latter section, relating to battered spouses and children, requires that the applicant not be "inadmissible" under section 212(a)(2) or "deportable" under section 237(a)(2) of the Act to be eligible for cancellation of removal. Based on the plain language of the statute, the petty offense exception should apply to battered spouses and children because a conviction for a *petty* offense that is a crime involving moral turpitude does not make an alien "inadmissible." *See* section 212(a)(2)(ii)(II) of the Act. However, section 240A(b)(1)(C) of the Act only requires that the applicant has not been convicted of an offense "under" sections 212(a)(2) or 237(a)(2) of the Act to be eligible for cancellation of removal. There is no reference to "inadmissible" or "deportable." For clarity, the language of section 240A(b)(1)(C) of the Act and section 240A(b)(2)(A)(iv) of the Act is as follows:

> (C) has not been convicted of an offense *under* section 212(a)(2), 237(a)(2), or 237(a)(3) . . .

See Section 240A(b)(1)(C) of the Act [Emphasis Added].

> (iv) the alien is not *inadmissible* under paragraph (2) or (3) of section 212(a), is not *deportable* under paragraphs (1)(G) or (2) through (4) of section 237(a) . . .

See Section 240A(b)(2)(A)(iv) of the Act [Emphasis Added].

The BIA did not distinguish the threshold requirements for battered spouses and children from the threshold requirements for all other aliens convicted of crimes involving moral turpitude. The BIA applies the petty offense exception to both classes, even though the language of the two operative paragraphs in the same section of law is very different. It seems impossible to reconcile application of the petty offense exception in the *Almanza*, *Cortez* and *Pedroza* decisions with the language Congress used to distinguish the eligibility requirements for battered spouses and children from all other aliens who have been convicted of crimes involving moral turpitude. Thus, the BIA has seems to have provided a windfall of eligibility for the cancellation of removal applicant convicted of a petty offense involving moral turpitude, even though such applicant is not a battered spouse or child.

The term, "moral turpitude," is not just difficult to interpret from English into most other languages. It is also difficult to define in English for immigration law purposes. Congress used this term to describe certain convicted aliens considered to be undesirables in the Act of March 3, 1891, and it has remained in our immigration statutes to this day. The BIA noted, in *Matter of Danesh*, 19 I&N Dec. 669 (BIA 1988), that moral turpitude is a "nebulous concept." The United States Supreme Court defined an act involving moral turpitude as:

> an act of baseness, vileness, or depravity in the private and social duties which a man owes to his fellow men or to society in general contrary to the accepted and customary rule of right and duty between man and man.

Jordan v. De George, 341 U.S. 223, reh'g denied 341 U.S. 956 (1951).

The BIA developed an objective approach to determine whether a crime involves moral turpitude. This approach is based on examination of the applicable statute and the record of conviction. *Matter of Esfandiary*, 16 I&N Dec. 659, 660-61 (BIA 1979). Essentially, the BIA's objective approach involves looking at the definition of an offense in the applicable penal code or statute and ultimately the records of the trial court that issued a conviction to determine the elements

Excuses For Criminal Behavior

"I knew the guns were stolen, but I didn't take possession of them. I just loaned $150 to the man who offered to sell them and told him to throw them in the trash."

The BIA has long held that knowing possession of stolen property is a crime involving moral turpitude. *Matter of Islam*, 25, I&N Dec. 637 (BIA 2011); *Matter of Salvail*, 17 I&N Dec. 19 (BIA 1979); *Matter of A-*, 7 I&N Dec. 626 (BIA 1957). At least one appellate court has determined that receiving stolen property with the subjective belief that it was stolen is a crime involving moral turpitude. *De Leon-Reynoso v. Ashcroft*, 293 F.3d 633 (3rd Cir. 2002). The United States Supreme Court upheld a conviction for possession of counterfeiting dies when willing and conscious possession is required. *Baender v. Barnett*, 255 U.S. 224 (1921). In criminal law, one of the more difficult elements of proof is knowledge. The author of this excuse readily admitted knowledge that the guns were stolen.

of the offense under consideration in immigration proceedings. Elements of an offense used in the context of this discussion mean the minimum facts and legal components necessary to prove the completion an offense. The idea behind this objective approach is to determine whether or not an offense is a crime involving moral turpitude based only on the specific elements that had to be proven in criminal court to obtain a conviction. For example, according to the BIA's objective approach, behavior described in a police report for which the respondent was *not* convicted is not relevant for the purpose of determining whether an offense for which the respondent *was* convicted is a crime involving moral turpitude. A conviction for a lesser included crime is another example. A criminal defendant indicted for murder might only be convicted for a reckless assault at the end of a criminal trial. The BIA's objective approach prohibits consideration of elements defining the offense of murder and only permits consideration of the elements that comprise reckless assault for classification purposes.

The BIA's objective approach was modified by Attorney General Michael Mukasey in November 2008 to include three consecutive tiers of inquiry. *Matter of Silva-Trevino*, 24 I&N Dec. 687 (A.G. 2008). To determine whether an offense is a crime involving moral turpitude, Immigration Judges should: 1) look at the statute to categorically determine whether there is a "realistic probability" that the offense includes conduct that does not involve moral turpitude; 2) if the categorical inquiry does not establish the classification of the offense as a categorical crime involving moral turpitude, engage in a modified categorical inquiry by examining the record of conviction; and 3) if the record of conviction does not conclusively establish the classification of the offense with regard to moral turpitude, consider any additional evidence deemed necessary to accurately determine whether or not the offense is a crime involving moral turpitude. *Matter of Silva-Trevino, supra.*

The third tier of the *Silva-Trevino* approach gave me cause for circumspection as an Immigration Judge. Opening the hearing to

Excuses For Criminal Behavior

"I didn't steal anything. I was with a friend who had a flat tire, and he got a tire from another car. We were changing the tire when the police came by, and they accused me with my friend."

Many people do not understand the law of parties. Generally, a person is liable as an accomplice if he or she assists or encourages another to commit a crime with the intent to facilitate the commission of the crime. *United States v. Frazier*, 880 F.2d 878, 886 (6th Cir. 1989), *cert. denied*, 493 U.S. 1053 (1990).

receive evidence from the parties about the whether the respondent's offense is a crime involving moral turpitude, after review of the statute and trial court record failed to answer the question, is like opening Pandora's box or at least a can of worms. What are the evidentiary limits? Should behavior for which the respondent was *not* convicted taint the offense as a crime involving moral turpitude? Should the respondent's good intentions while committing the offense characterize the offense? There is a danger in the application of the third tier of the *Silva-Trevino* approach for Immigration Judges and the parties to embark on a re-trial of a criminal matter in a civil setting and to overlook the requirement that an alien (for virtually all immigration disabling provisions that I can imagine) must not only *commit* a crime involving moral turpitude. The alien must be *convicted* for a crime involving moral turpitude. In any event, once a third tier *Silva-Trevino* inquiry is launched it will be a long day for all participants involved in the hearing, as well as for those involved in the appellate process.

In my experience, review of the criminal charging document (i.e. indictment or information) almost always resolved the moral turpitude question. In fact, the criminal charging document is, in my opinion, the best place to look to determine what basket of elements define the offense for which a respondent had been convicted. Ordinarily, there should be no need to look anywhere else. Of course, the need to look elsewhere becomes obvious when the criminal charging document is not available. In Harris County, Texas, for example, charging documents are deleted from the court records after a specific number of years.

As you can see, application of the law relating to crimes involving moral turpitude almost always involves shades of gray rather than clearly defined black and white concepts. However, those who crave clarity might be consoled to know that the BIA has consistently considered theft to be a crime involving moral turpitude. *Matter of V-*, 1 I&N Dec. 340 (BIA 1945); *Matter of V-I-*, 3 I&N Dec. 571, 572 (BIA 1949); *Matter of Garcia*, 11 I&N Dec. 521, 523 (BIA 1966); *Matter of*

APPROACHING THE BENCH FROM INSIDE THE IMMIGRATION COURT

Scarpulla, 15 I&N Dec. 139, at 140-41 (BIA 1974). *See also Chiarmonte v. INS*, 626 F.2d 1093, 1097 (2nd Cir. 1980).

Hardship

Applicants for cancellation of removal who are not battered spouses or children must establish exceptional and extremely unusual hardship to a qualifying relative (i.e. United States citizen or lawful permanent resident spouse, parent or child) arising from the applicant's removal from the United States. A specific test for exceptional and extremely unusual hardship does not exist. The BIA, however, has determined that exceptional and extremely unusual hardship is hardship beyond what has been historically required in suspension of deportation cases under section 244(a)(1) of the former Act (before enactment of IIRIRA on September 30, 1996). Applicants for suspension of deportation were required to establish *extreme hardship*, as opposed to *exceptional and extremely unusual hardship*. Currently, applicants who are battered spouses or children are bound by the more relaxed extreme hardship standard of the historical suspension of deportation provision. The Immigration Judge can also consider hardship to the applicant who is a battered spouse or child as well as the applicant's qualifying relatives (i.e. the alien's child or, if the alien is a child, the alien's parent). *See* section 240A(b)(2)(A)(v) of the Act. To establish exceptional and extremely unusual hardship, an applicant for cancellation of removal must demonstrate that at least one of his or her qualifying relatives would suffer hardship that is substantially beyond the hardship which would ordinarily be expected to result from deportation. However, it is not necessary for the applicant to establish unconscionable hardship. *Matter of Monreal*, 23 I&N Dec. 56 (BIA 2001).

The BIA identified specific factors to consider when making hardship determinations. *Matter of Anderson*, 16 I&N Dec. 596 (BIA 1978). In the *Anderson* decision, the BIA addressed *extreme hardship* in the context of a suspension of deportation application under section 244(a)(1) of the former Act (before enactment of IIRIRA on September 30, 1996). The specific hardship factors identified by the BIA in the *Anderson* decision are as follows:

1) the age of the applicant;
2) family ties in the United States and abroad;
3) length of residence in the United States;
4) state of health;
5) economic and political conditions in the country to which the applicant is returnable;
6) financial status, including business and occupation;
7) the possibility of other means of adjustment;
8) special assistance to the United States or the applicant's community; and
9) immigration history.

See also Matter of O-J-O-, 21 I&N Dec. 381 (BIA 1996). Not all of the hardship factors identified in the *Anderson* decision are relevant to an application for cancellation of removal, because hardship the applicant (except battered spouses and children) cannot be considered, except to the extent that it affects hardship to a qualifying relative. *Matter of Monreal, supra.* I believe that the best way to make a determination about exceptional and extremely unusual hardship is to align the circumstances surrounding each of the qualifying relatives (including the applicant if a battered spouse or child) with the *Anderson* hardship factors, make an assessment about the severity of the hardship and decide whether or not the hardship individually or cumulatively falls outside of the ordinary hardships that occur when an alien is removed from the United States. A good example of how the BIA analyzes hardship can be found in *Matter of Pilch,* 21 I&N Dec. 627 (BIA 1996) (addressing extreme hardship under section 241(a)(1) of the former Act before enactment of IIRIRA on September 30, 1996). *See also Matter of Monreal, supra; Matter of Andazola,* 23 I&N Dec. 319 (BIA 2002); *Matter of Recinas,* 23, I&N Dec. 467 (BIA 2002). In

Matter of Pilch, the BIA decided that a husband and wife who were citizens of Poland failed to demonstrate individual or cumulative factors that demonstrate "extreme hardship over and above the normal economic and social disruptions involved in deportation" to themselves or to their 3 United States citizen children. In *Matter of Monreal*, the BIA determined that the respondent did not establish exceptional and extremely unusual hardship for his 2 children who were 8 and 12 years of age. The respondent in *Matter of Monreal* was a 34 year old citizen of Mexico who had been living in the United States for approximately 20 years beginning at 14 years of age. The respondent's parents and 7 siblings were residing lawfully in the United States. One of the respondent's siblings lived in Mexico, and the respondent's wife lived in Mexico. In *Matter of Andazola*, the BIA held that an unmarried mother failed to establish that her two children who were 6 and 11 years of age would suffer exceptional and extremely unusual hardship upon her removal to Mexico, in spite of poor economic conditions, diminished educational opportunities in Mexico and the fact that the respondent was unmarried and had no family in Mexico to assist her upon her return with her children. In *Matter of Recinas*, the BIA determined that a single mother who had no immediate family in Mexico and was the only source of support for 6 children established exceptional and extremely unusual hardship to 4 United States children who were 5, 8, 11, and 12 years of age and who were unfamiliar with Spanish.

In my experience adjudicating cancellation of removal applications, current interpretation of the law often disfavors applicants who have achieved higher levels of success by establishing a business or accumulating assets in the United States. For example, the BIA in *Matter of Pilch*, at 631, reasoned that the loss of the respondent's business, "although unfortunate, does not entail extreme economic hardship, but instead, is a normal occurrence when an alien is deported." The BIA noted in *Matter of Andazola*, at 324, that the respondent owned a home and 2 vehicles, participated in a retirement plan, and had saved about $7000, but reasoned that "the respondent and her children would not be penniless upon her return to Mexico. The money she does have would surely help her in establishing a new life in Mexico."

One of my colleagues who preceded me in retirement sometimes tried to assuage the pain of a denied cancellation of removal application by telling the applicant that he or she would not want the kind of hardship that would qualify the applicant for relief.

Ineligible Aliens

The following aliens are not eligible for cancellation of removal as a matter of law:

1) aliens who entered the United States as a crewman subsequent to June 30, 1964;
2) aliens who were admitted or became exchange visitors under section 101(a)(15)(J) of the Act in order to receive a graduate medical degree or training;
3) aliens who were admitted or became exchange visitors under section 100(a)(15)(J) of the Act other than to receive a graduate medical degree or training, and are subject to the 2 year foreign residency requirement without having obtained a waiver or fulfilled the requirement;
4) aliens who are inadmissible under section 212(a)(3) of the Act or deportable under section 237(a)(4) of the Act (security or terrorist related grounds);
5) aliens who participated in the persecution of others under section 241(b)(3)(B)(i) of the Act; and
6) aliens who have been granted cancellation of removal, suspension of deportation, or a waiver under section 212(c) of the Act in past.

See section 240A(c) of the Act.

Suspension of Deportation

Suspension of deportation is the precursor of cancellation of removal, but occasionally it is still available to respondents in deportation proceedings. Deportation proceedings are immigration court proceedings initiated before the consolidation of deportation and exclusion proceedings into removal proceedings that took effect after enactment of IIRIRA on September 30, 1996. Believe it or not, a number of pending deportation and exclusion proceedings that were initiated before September 30, 1996 still exist. Like cancellation of removal, suspension of deportation is a discretionary form of relief. *Matter of Turcotte*, 12 I&N Dec. 206 (BIA 1967).

To be eligible for suspension of deportation under section 244(a)(1) of the former Act, an applicant must prove that:

1) the applicant has been present in the United States for 7 years immediately preceding the date of the application;
2) the applicant has been a person of good moral character for the same 7 year period; and
3) the applicant's deportation will result in extreme hardship to the applicant or to the applicant's United States citizen or lawful permanent resident spouse, children, or parents.

An alien who is deportable under paragraphs (2), (3), or (4) of section 241(a) of the former Act (criminals, document fraud, national security and related grounds) is eligible to apply for suspension of deportation under section 244(a)(2) of the former Act. To be eligible for suspension of deportation under section 244(a)(2) of the former Act, an applicant must prove:

1) continuous physical presence in the United States for at least 10 years immediately following the event which gave rise to one or more of the grounds for deportation identified above and immediately preceding the application for suspension of deportation; *Matter of P-*, 6 I&N Dec. 788 (BIA 1955); *Matter of Lozada*, 19 I&N Dec. 637 (BIA 1988);
2) good moral character for at least 10 years immediately

preceding the application for suspension of deportation; *Matter of M-*, 5 I&N Dec. 261 (BIA 1953); and

3) that deportation would cause exceptional and extremely unusual hardship to the applicant or the applicant's United States citizen or lawful permanent resident spouse, parent or child.

An alien who has been battered or subjected to extreme cruelty in the United States by a United States citizen or lawful permanent resident spouse, or parent of a child who has been battered or subjected to extreme cruelty, is eligible to apply for suspension of deportation under section 244(a)(3) of the former Act (before enactment of IIRIRA on September 30, 1996), provided:

1) the applicant is not deportable under section 241(a)(1)(G) or paragraphs (2), (3), or (4) of section 241 of the former Act (marriage fraud, criminals, document fraud, or security or related grounds);

2) the applicant has been physically present in the United States for at least 3 years immediately preceding the application date;

3) the applicant has been a person of good moral character for the same 3 year period; and

4) deportation would result in extreme hardship to the applicant or the applicant's parent or child.

Physical Presence

It is important to remember that section 309(c)(5) of IIRIRA as amended by section 203(a) of the Nicaraguan and Central American Relief Act of 1997 ("NACARA") provides that the same continuous presence provisions that apply to cancellation of removal applications also apply to suspension of deportation applications because they apply "before, on, or after" September 30, 1996, the day that IIRIRA was enacted. In other words, physical presence is cut off upon service of the Notice to Appear (Form I-862) or the Order to Show Cause (Form I-221). *Matter of Nolasco*, supra. For more technical discussion about the effective date of IIRIRA, see *Matter of N-J-B-*, 21 I&N Dec. 812 (BIA 1997).

Hardship

The same hardship factors discussed in connection with cancellation of removal apply to hardship determinations relating to suspension of deportation. Before the enactment of IIRIRA, the BIA had determined that a respondent who had filed a motion to reopen to apply for suspension of deportation under section 244(a)(2) of the former Act established a *prima facie* showing of exceptional and extremely unusual hardship by demonstrating the following facts:

1) the respondent was a lawful permanent resident who was 45 years of age and had spent almost half of his 45 years in the United States;
2) steady employment;
3) immediate family, including his wife and 2 United States citizen children were well established in the United States;
4) one United States citizen child was undergoing treatment for a congenital heart defect; and
5) the respondent's drug conviction rendered the respondent ineligible for any other form of relief, and precluded him from legally immigrating to the United States in the future.

Matter of Pena-Diaz, 20 I&N Dec. 841, at 845 (BIA 1994). If the DHS placed an alien in the same circumstances as Pena-Diaz in removal proceedings (as opposed to deportation proceedings) the alien would not be eligible for cancellation of removal due to an absolute bar to relief arising from his drug conviction (i.e. a conviction under section 212(a)(2) and/or section 237(a)(2) of the Act). *Matter of Cortez*, 25 I&N Dec. 301 (BIA 2010).

Ineligible Aliens

The following classes of aliens are not eligible for suspension of deportation:

1) aliens who entered the United States as a crewman after June 30, 1964;
2) aliens who were admitted as exchange visitors under section 101(a)(15)(J) of the Act in order to receive a graduate medical degree or training; and
3) aliens who were admitted or became exchange visitors under section 101(a)(15)(J) of the Act other than to receive a graduate medical degree or training, and are subject to the 2 year foreign residency requirement without having obtained a waiver or fulfilled the requirement.

Comparison of the requirements for suspension of deportation to the requirements for cancellation of removal reveals that it is generally easier to qualify for suspension of deportation because:

1) hardship to the applicant can be considered;
2) conviction for a crime involving moral turpitude or drug crime does not absolutely bar relief;
3) exclusion grounds do not apply;
4) a conviction for an aggravated felony does not absolutely bar relief;
5) being inadmissible or deportable for security or terrorist grounds does not absolutely bar relief;
6) participation in the persecution of others does not absolutely bar relief; and
7) a past grant of cancellation of removal or suspension of deportation or a waiver under section 212(c) of the former Act does not absolutely bar relief.

The following work sheet based on the *Anderson* factors can be useful for preparation in anticipation of an immigration court hearing relating to a cancellation of removal or suspension of deportation application. The *Anderson* factors can be adapted to

APPROACHING THE BENCH FROM INSIDE THE IMMIGRATION COURT

the circumstances of qualifying relatives (i.e. United States citizen or lawful permanent resident spouse, parent, or child). It is important to identify family members who are not qualifying relatives. The existence of family members in the United States and abroad commonly affect hardship to qualifying relatives whether or not the qualifying relatives will accompany the applicant outside the United States if the applicant is deported or removed.

WILLIAM K. ZIMMER

Suspension/Cancellation of Removal Worksheet

I. Age (age related disabilities, etc.):

II. Family Ties (United States and abroad, including families of spouses and ex-spouses and parents of children who are qualifying relatives):

III. Length of Residence in the United States (assimilation):
   A. Include history of respondent's arrival(s) in the United States.
   B. Note time of service of the Order to Show Cause or Notice to Appear (physical presence cut off).

IV. Health:

V. Economic and Political Conditions in Home Country:

APPROACHING THE BENCH FROM INSIDE THE IMMIGRATION COURT

VI. Financial Status:
- A. Income
- B. Property
    - a. Real Property
    - b. Personal Property

VII. Other Means of Adjustment (favored over suspension or cancellation of removal as a matter of discretion):

VIII. Special Assistance to the United States/Community:

IX. Immigration History:

X. Criminal History:

Number Cap

Congress imposed an annual cap on the number of cancellation of removal and suspension of deportation applications that can be granted in any fiscal year. Specifically, only 4,000 applications for cancellation of removal and suspension of deportation in the aggregate can be granted in any fiscal year. *See* section 240A(e)(1) of the Act. The application of this number cap requires Immigration Judges to hold hearings relating to cancellation of removal and suspension of deportation applications, even if the 4,000 number cap has been reached. However, after the 4,000 number cap has been reached the Immigration Judge must reserve decision noting the date and time of the hearing completion, unless the respondent is not eligible for relief as a matter of law. A decision cannot be granted or denied based on a determination of hardship, good moral character (unless specifically barred under section 101(f) of the Act), or any exercise of discretion. *See* 8 C.F.R. § 1240.21(c)(1). For example, after the 4,000 number cap is reached and the Immigration Judge determines that the applicant is not eligible for cancellation of removal because the applicant cannot establish 10 years of continuous physical presence required under section 240A(b)(1)(A) of the Act or the applicant is not eligible for relief because the applicant has committed a crime that triggers a bar to relief under section 240A(b)(1)(C) of the Act, the Immigration Judge *may* issue a decision denying the application. On the other hand, if the Immigration Judge determines that the applicant cannot establish exceptional and extremely unusual hardship to one or more of the applicant's qualifying relatives after the 4,000 number cap has been reached the Immigration Judge *cannot* issue a decision granting or denying the application. Once the 4,000 number cap has been lifted (i.e. the arrival of a new fiscal year), the reserved decisions will be issued in oral or written form in chronological order. Numbers will be subtracted from the new 4,000 number cap and used for reserved decisions in chronological order based on the completion date and time of the last hearing as noted by the Immigration Judge. When the 4,000 number cap is reached in the new fiscal year, Immigration Judges will again begin reserving decisions, noting the date and time of the concluded hearing. As a matter of simple addition and subtraction, it is possible for numbers to become back logged so that at the beginning of each fiscal year the 4,000 number cap is reached as soon as the new numbers become available. An applicant with a strong application will want to complete his or her hearing as soon as possible to reserve a place in line for the use of a number that will enable the Immigration Judge to issue a decision.

Relief Under the Nicaraguan and Central American Relief Act of 1997

Specific classes of aliens described in the Nicaraguan and Central American Relief Act of 1997 ("NACARA") are eligible to apply for suspension of deportation or special rule cancellation of removal. These classes of aliens include:

1) a registered ABC class member who has not been apprehended at the time of entry to the United States after December 19, 1990;
2) a Guatemalan or El Salvadoran National who filed an application for asylum on or before April 1, 1990;
3) a national of the Soviet Union, Russia, any republic of the Soviet Union, Latvia, Estonia, Lithuania, Poland, Czechoslovakia, Romania, Hungary, Bulgaria, Albania, East Germany, Yugoslavia, or any state of the former Yugoslavia who entered the United States on or before December 31, 1991;
4) an alien spouse or child of any of the above described aliens at the time a special rule suspension of deportation or cancellation of removal application is granted;
5) an alien unmarried son or daughter of any of the aliens

described above in 1), 2) , and 3) who is 21 years or older at the time a special rule suspension of deportation or cancellation of removal application is granted, and entered the United States on or before October 1, 1990.

An ABC class member is a class member in *American Baptist Churches v. Thornburgh*, 760 F. Supp. 796 (N.D. Cal 1991). Specifically the class includes any Guatemalan national who first entered the United States on or before October 1, 1990 and any El Salvadoran National who entered the United States on or before September 19, 1990. These class members are the beneficiaries of a settlement agreement with the United States government.

The same threshold criteria for suspension of deportation under section 244(a) of the former Act apply to special rule suspension of deportation and cancellation of removal under the NACARA. However, primary beneficiaries of the NACARA who are ABC class members and Guatemalan and El Salvadoran nationals (described above under "1" and "2") enjoy a rebuttable presumption of extreme hardship. *See* 8 C.F.R. § 1240.64(d). This is a major advantage for such applicants. Extreme hardship is often the most difficult requirement that an applicant must prove, and the DHS must establish that "it is more likely than not that neither the applicant nor a qualified relative would suffer extreme hardship if the applicant were deported or removed from the United States" to rebut the presumption. *See* 8 C.F.R. § 1240.64(d)(3). Nevertheless, family members of Guatemalan and El Salvadoran primary beneficiaries as well as the Eastern European nationals do not enjoy the presumption of extreme hardship. In the context of this discussion of the NACARA, a primary beneficiary is an alien who directly benefits from the NACARA provisions as opposed to an alien who derives benefits through another alien as a family member.

The 4,000 number cap discussed above for cancellation of removal and suspension of deportation applications does not apply aliens who are eligible to apply for relief under the NACARA. *See* section 240A(e)(3)(A) of the Act.

Chapter V

Legitimation of Immigration Status

Adjustment of Status

"Adjustment of status" is a term of art in United States immigration law. It usually denotes a change from temporary immigration status or no immigration status to lawful permanent resident status under section 245 of the Act. Aliens can also adjust from one temporary immigration status to another temporary immigration status. However, the phrase adjustment of status is sometimes used loosely outside of the context of section 245 of the Act. For example, the subject heading relating to cancellation of removal is as follows: "Cancellation of Removal and Adjustment of Status for Certain Nonpermanent Residents." *See* section 240A(b) of the Act. I have witnessed confusion on the part of some immigration attorneys who made misguided attempts to treat cancellation of removal like adjustment of status under section 245 of the Act. This confusion was manifested by filing exclusion waivers and even visa petitions with cancellation of removal applications and otherwise misapplying the criteria for adjustment of status under section 245 of the Act. In short, the phrase "adjustment of status" does not have the same technical meaning everywhere it appears in the immigration law.

An applicant for adjustment of status under section 245(a) of the Act must have been inspected and admitted or paroled into the United States. In addition, the applicant must:

1) be eligible to receive an immigrant visa;
2) be admissible to the United States for lawful permanent residence (which means that the applicant cannot be inadmissible under *any* provision of section 212(a) of the Act); and
3) an immigrant visa must be immediately available at the time the adjustment application is filed.

See 8 C.F.R. § 1245.1.

Eligible to Receive an Immigrant Visa

Generally, to be eligible to receive an immigrant visa, an applicant for adjustment of status under section 245(a) of the Act must meet the requirements for an immigrant visa described under section 201 of the Act. These immigrant visas are available to two broad categories of aliens; family sponsored immigrants and employment based immigrants. The applicant must not be subject to numerical limitations set forth in sections 201 and 202 of the Act; a visa number must be allocated for the applicant under section 203 of the Act; and the applicant must meet all of the procedural requirements imposed under section 204 of the Act (i.e. procedures governing visa petitions). *See* 8 C.F.R. Part 204.

Be Admissible to the United States

Since an alien applying for adjustment of status must be admissible to the United States as an immigrant, the BIA has determined that "an alien applying for adjustment of status under section 245 is assimilated to the position of an alien who is making an entry." *Matter of Connelly*, 19 I&N Dec. 156, at 159 (BIA 1984). Section 212(a) of the Act describes all of the categories of aliens who are inadmissible or subject to exclusion from the United States. For example, a common ground of inadmissibility that is raised in connection with adjustment of status during immigration proceedings is section 212(a)(2)(A)(i)(I) of the Act (conviction for a crime involving moral turpitude). An applicant for adjustment of status under section 245 of the Act, who is inadmissible under any section of 212(a) of the Act, may apply for a waiver of the ground of inadmissibility if a statutory provision for such waiver exists. *Matter of Alarcon*, 20 I&N Dec. 557 (BIA 1992). *See* 8 C.F.R. § 1240.11(a)(2).

Immigrant Visa Must be Immediately Available

An immediately available visa means that an immigrant visa has been approved and is not encumbered by numerical limitation. For example, an approved visa for the spouse of a United States citizen has no numerical limitation and is immediately available. However, only a limited number of immigrant visas for spouses of lawful permanent residents can be issued in any one year. Therefore, an immigrant visa for the spouse of a lawful permanent resident may be approved, but it may not be available until the priority date for such visa becomes current. The date that a visa petition is filed reserves the beneficiary's place in the line of visa petitions filed in that category. The earlier the visa petition is filed the earlier a visa number will become available. In short, an approved immigrant visa petition without a current priority date (if visa numbers are limited) means that a visa is *not* immediately available. Consequently, the beneficiary of the visa petition without a current priority date is not eligible for adjustment of status under section 245 of the Act. The United States State Department publishes monthly visa bulletins containing the current priority dates for various visa categories and countries.

One misconception that occasionally arises in immigration proceedings is the notion that an approved immigrant visa petition and an immigrant visa are equivalent. An immigrant visa and an immigrant visa petition are two entirely different and independent documents. The former is a travel document issued by a United States consulate office outside the United States after an approved visa petition has been forwarded to the consulate office for that purpose. The latter is an application for an immigrant visa. For the purpose of adjustment of status under section 245 of the Act, an approved visa petition with a current priority date is treated like an immigrant visa. Adjustment of status circumvents the procedure for immigrant visa processing at a United States consulate office by not requiring the beneficiary of the visa petition to depart from the United States to obtain an immigrant visa. If consular processing is utilized the immigrant visa is issued to the beneficiary abroad, who uses the immigrant visa as a travel document to return to the United States. I have witnessed immigration attorneys mistakenly assert that their client is not inadmissible because he or she is in possession of an approved immigrant visa petition. Typically, this assertion is made in an effort to avoid an exclusion charge under section 212(a)(7)(A)(i)(I) of the Act (immigrant applying for admission to the United States without an immigrant visa or other suitable travel document). On more than one occasion DHS attorneys have argued to me that consular processing is the equivalent of adjustment of status in an attempt to persuade me that no prejudice would arise from denial of an adjustment application. It appears that the confusion can be attributed to the failure to distinguish between the nature of adjustment of status and the nature of consular processing. Adjustment of status is a form of relief from removal. Consular processing is not. Adjustment of status yields benefits for the Department of State as well as the applicant for adjustment of status, by reducing the work load of the United States consulate offices overseas.

Aliens Ineligible For Adjustment of Status

The following categories of aliens are ineligible for adjustment of status under section 245 of the Act, unless the alien establishes eligibility under section 245(i) of the Act:

1) alien crewmen;
2) aliens who worked in the United States without authorization

prior to filing an application for adjustment of status or who failed to continuously maintain lawful immigration status after entry to the United States, except for *immediate relatives* (section 201(b) of the Act) and *special immigrants* (section 101(a)(27)(H), (I), (J), or (K) of the Act);

3) aliens admitted in transit without visa under section 212(d)(4)(C) of the Act;

4) aliens, other than immediate relatives defined under section 201(b) of the Act, admitted as nonimmigrant visitors without a visa under sections 212(l) or 217 of the Act;

5) aliens admitted as nonimmigrants described in section 101(a)(15)(S) of the Act (i.e. aliens determined to have critical reliable information about a criminal organization or enterprise, who are willing to cooperate with an authorized criminal investigation or prosecution);

6) aliens who are deportable under section 237(a)(4)(B) of the Act (terrorist activities);

7) aliens applying for employment based immigrant status (under section 203(b) of the Act) who are not in lawful nonimmigrant status;

8) aliens who were employed while having the status of an unauthorized alien (defined under section 274A(h)(3) of the Act) or who had otherwise violated the terms of nonimmigrant status.

See section 245(c) of the Act.

Adjustment of Status Under Section 245(i) of the Act

An applicant for adjustment of status under section 245(i) of the Act must:

1) be physically in the United States;

2) have entered the United States without inspection or fall within the categories of aliens identified under section 245(c)

of the Act as not eligible for adjustment of status under section 245(a) of the Act;

3) be eligible to receive an immigrant visa and be admissible to the United States (i.e. not inadmissible under section 212(a) of the Act);

4) pay a sum of $1000 upon filing the adjustment application (except for children under 17 years of age and spouses or unmarried children of legalized aliens who entered and resided in the United States as of May 5, 1988 and applied for *Family Unity* benefits (i.e. temporary stay of deportation and work authorization) under section 301 of the Immigration Act of 1990); *Matter of Fesale*, 21 I&N Dec. 114 (BIA 1995);

5) have an immediately available immigrant visa;

6) have filed an immigrant visa petition or labor certification on or before April 30, 2001; and

7) establish physical presence in the United States on December 21, 2000 (the enactment date of the LIFE Act amendments of 2000).

Aliens who are deportable under section 237(a)(4)(B) of the Act for terrorist activities are not eligible for adjustment of status under section 245(i) of the Act, even though such aliens are listed in section 245(c) of the Act. *See* 8 C.F.R. § 1245.10(g). Eligibility for an immigrant visa, being admissible (i.e. not inadmissible under section 212(a) of the Act) and immediate availability of an immigrant visa, which are all required for adjustment of status under section 245(a) of the Act, are also required for adjustment of status under section 245(i) of the Act.

An applicant who meets the statutory requirements for adjustment of status under section 245 of the Act is not entitled to discretionary relief. Adjustment of status is a matter of administrative grace, and may be granted or denied in the exercise of discretion. *Hintopoulos v. Shaughnessy*, 353 U.S. 72 (1957). In the absence of adverse circumstances, adjustment of status should be granted. In the presence of past misconduct, however, an applicant's equities must be sufficient to overcome such misconduct. *Matter of Blas*,

APPROACHING THE BENCH FROM INSIDE THE IMMIGRATION COURT

15 I&N Dec. 626 (BIA 1974; A.G. 1976). In the presence of serious adverse factors, a showing of unusual or outstanding equities may be required. *Matter of Arai*, 13 I&N Dec. 494 (BIA 1970).

Jurisdiction Over Arriving Aliens

An Immigration Judge does not have jurisdiction to adjudicate an adjustment application filed by an arriving alien unless:

1) the alien properly filed the application for adjustment with the former INS or the DHS while the arriving alien was in the United States (i.e. prior to the alien's last departure);
2) the alien returned to the United States pursuant to a grant of advance parole to pursue the previously filed adjustment application;
3) the application for adjustment of status was denied by the former INS or the DHS; and
4) the DHS placed the alien in removal proceedings upon the alien's application to return to the United States pursuant to a grant of advanced parole, or placed the alien in removal proceedings after the DHS denied the adjustment application.

See 8 C.F.R. § 1245.2(a)(1)(ii).

The phrase, "arriving alien," is a term of art in United States immigration law that describes an alien who is applying for admission to the United States upon arrival from a foreign port or place. The term also includes aliens who have been paroled into the United States. Even though a paroled alien is physically in the United States, the parole status preserves the alien's posture as an applicant for admission. *See* section 212(d)(5)(A) of the Act. Supreme Court Justice Sandra O'Conner discussed different immigration procedures that affected excludable (arriving) aliens and deportable aliens. *See Landon v. Plascencia*, 459 U.S. 21 (1982). *Landon v. Plascencia* was decided before the September 30, 1996 enactment of IIRIRA. However, Justice O'Conner's discussion provides insight about the procedural dichotomy based on classification of aliens as excludable (inadmissible) aliens and deportable aliens. This dichotomy persists in immigration law, even after the elimination of exclusion and deportation hearings in favor of removal proceedings by the enactment of IIRIRA. The reader might recall from the history in chapter I that exclusion of aliens was the sole means of immigration law enforcement until after 1880.

Child Status Protection Act

Congress passed the Child Status Protection Act ("CSPA") on August 6, 2002 in response to the apparent hardships and inequity caused by delay on the part of the former INS and the DHS in adjudicating visa petitions. The age of an alien beneficiary of a visa petition determines whether or not the alien is a child defined in part under section 101(b)(1) of the Act as "an unmarried person under twenty-one years of age . . ." Since classification as a child is essential for certain visa categories, such as immediate relative status and children of lawful permanent residents, experience teaches that these beneficiaries risk aging out of their child status while waiting for the DHS to make a decision about their visa petition. Therefore, the primary purpose for the CSPA is to eliminate the risk of aging out of child status by subtracting the elapsed time attributable to the DHS adjudication delay from the age of the visa petition beneficiary.

Section 201(f) of the Act (added by section 2 of the CSPA) provides rules for determining immediate relative status. The general rule for determining whether an alien beneficiary is a child (i.e. under 21 years of age) and is therefore an immediate relative, is to use the age of the alien on the visa petition filing date. Sometimes, a visa petitioner who is the parent of an alien child beneficiary naturalizes to become a United States citizen. In this circumstance, the age on

APPROACHING THE BENCH FROM INSIDE THE IMMIGRATION COURT

the date of naturalization is used to determine whether the alien beneficiary is a child (i.e. under 21 years of age) and is therefore an immediate relative of the naturalized visa petitioner. Sometimes a conversion of a married son or daughter to an immediate relative occurs upon termination of the marriage. In this circumstance, the age on the date of marriage termination is used to determine whether the alien beneficiary is a child (i.e. under 21 years of age) and is therefore an immediate relative of the petitioner.

Spouses or children of Lawful Permanent residents described under section 203(a)(2)(A) of the Act and aliens following to join a parent described under section 203(d) of the Act are addressed at section 203(h) of the Act, added by section 3 of the CSPA. Under section 203(h) of the Act, the age of the alien beneficiary at the time a visa number becomes available is used to determine whether the alien is a child under section 101(b)(1) of the Act (i.e. under 21 years of age). A visa is deemed to become available when:

1) the visa is approved, and
2) the visa number becomes available (i.e. the priority date becomes current).

The alien beneficiary must apply for admission or adjustment of status within 1 year of the day the visa number becomes available. If all of the above described conditions are met the age of the alien beneficiary is reduced by the time that elapsed while the visa petition was pending. It is important to remember that the time lapse between the visa adjudication date and the day that the visa number becomes available does *not* reduce the alien beneficiary's age.

The effective date for the CSPA is August 6, 2002 (the CSPA enactment date). The CSPA applies to alien beneficiaries whose:

1) visa petitions were approved before August 6, 2002 only if a *final* determination has not been made on the application for an immigrant visa *or adjustment of status*; and
2) the visa petition is pending on or after August 6, 2002; or
3) the application for adjustment of status or an immigrant

visa is pending before the Department of Justice or the Department of State on or after August 6, 2002. *See* section 8 of the CSPA.

Adjustment of Status Under the Cuban Adjustment Act of 1966

Regardless of the ineligibility provisions in section 245(c) of the Act, any alien who is a native and citizen of Cuba is eligible for adjustment to lawful permanent resident status in the United States if the applicant:

1) was inspected and admitted or paroled into the United States subsequent to January 1, 1959;
2) has been physically present in the United States for at least 1 year;
3) is eligible to receive an immigrant visa; and
4) is admissible to the United States for permanent residence.

In my experience, most adjustments of Cuban Nationals in the United States occur under the authority of the Cuban Adjustment Act of 1966. The threshold requirements are very relaxed compared to the requirements for legitimation of immigration status under other statutes. Even after a Cuban national enters the United States without inspection (making him or her ineligible for adjustment under the Cuban Adjustment Act of 1966), the DHS often paroles such alien into the United States *after* apprehension, curing ineligibility for adjustment under the Cuban Adjustment Act of 1966. The Cuban government has a history of refusing repatriation of its citizens unless the Cuban citizen is listed in an agreement with the United States following the 1980 Mariel Cuban boat lift. It should be noted that currently, the immigration court does not usually have jurisdiction over adjustment applications under the Cuban Adjustment Act of 1966 due to a change in jurisdictional interpretation by the BIA. *Matter of Martinez-Montalvo*, 24 I&N Dec. 778 (BIA 2009).

Adjustment of Status Under the NACARA

An applicant for adjustment of status under section 202(a) of the NACARA must be a national of Cuba or Nicaragua. In addition, the applicant must:

1) prove physical presence in the United States beginning on or before December 1, 1995, or be a spouse or child of an alien granted adjustment under section 202(a) of the NACARA; and

2) be admissible to the United States, except the following exclusion grounds do not apply:

    a) section 212(a)(4) of the Act (likely to become a public charge);

    b) section 212(a)(5) of the Act (lack of labor certification);

    c) section 212 (a)(6)(A) of the Act (present without admission or parole);

    d) section 212(a)(7)(A) of the Act (lack of immigrant visa or document);

    e) section 212(a)(9)(B) of the Act (aliens unlawfully present).

An unmarried son or daughter of an alien granted adjustment under section 202(a) of the NACARA is eligible for adjustment of status under the same section if he or she establishes continuous physical presence in the United States beginning on or before December 1, 1995.

Physical Presence

Under section 202(b)(1) of the NACARA, an alien shall be considered to have maintained continuous physical presence in the United States as long as any absence from the United States does not exceed 180 days and any absences from the United States do not exceed 180 days in the aggregate.

To prove continuous physical presence in the United States on or before December 1, 1995 under section 202(b)(2) of the NACARA, an applicant must demonstrate that prior to December 1, 1995 the applicant:

1) applied for asylum;
2) was issued an order to show cause;
3) was placed in exclusion proceedings;
4) applied for adjustment of status under section 245 of the Act;
5) applied for employment authorization;
6) performed service or engaged in trade or business in the United States recorded by the Commissioner of Social Security; or
7) applied for any other benefit under the Act;

Document requirements for proof of continuous physical presence in the United States for the purpose of a NACARA adjustment application are explicit and extensive. *See* 8 C.F.R. § 1245.13(e). It is not unusual for applications to fail for lack of documentation of continuous physical presence in the United States on or before December 1, 1995.

Adjustment of Status For Aliens Granted Asylum

Congress has given aliens who have been granted asylum in the United States an opportunity to adjust to lawful permanent resident status. *See* section 209 of the Act. To be eligible for adjustment of status under section 209(b) of the Act, an alien who has been granted asylum must apply for such relief and must establish that:

1) the alien has been physically present in the United States for at least 1 year after being granted asylum;
2) the alien continues to be a refugee under section 101(a)(42)(A) of the Act;
3) the alien is not firmly resettled in any foreign country; and
4) the alien is admissible to the United States as an immigrant

APPROACHING THE BENCH FROM INSIDE THE IMMIGRATION COURT

(i.e. not subject to any grounds of inadmissibility under section 212(a) of the Act).

Exclusion grounds under section 212(a)(4), (5), and (7)(A) (aliens likely to become a public charge, aliens lacking labor certification, and aliens lacking entry documents) do not apply to aliens seeking adjustment under section 209 of the Act.

Section 209(c) of the Act confers discretionary authority to the Attorney General of the United States (including the DHS) to waive exclusion grounds under section 212(a) of the Act for humanitarian purposes, to assure family unity, or when it is otherwise in the public interest. *See* 8 C.F.R. §§ 1209.1 (relating to refugees) and 1209.2 (relating to aliens granted asylum). However, sections 212(a)(2)(C) (relating to controlled substance traffickers) and 212(a)(3)(A), (B), (C), and (E) of the Act (relating to aliens classified as spies, saboteurs, terrorists, and aliens whose admission would cause serious foreign policy consequences for the United States, and aliens who participated in Nazi persecutions or genocide) may not be waived.

The BIA held that the Immigration Judge and the BIA had exclusive jurisdiction to consider a waiver of inadmissibility under section 209(c) of the Act once the DHS places an asylee in removal proceedings. The BIA also held that termination of asylum status is not mandatory if a respondent is eligible to apply for a 209(c) waiver. *See Matter of K-A-*, 23 I&N Dec. 661 (BIA 2004), where the DHS challenged the jurisdiction of the Immigration Judge to consider a waiver under section 209(c) of the Act, asserting that the DHS had exclusive jurisdiction. According to *Matter of K-A-*, an Immigration Judge also has jurisdiction to consider a 209(c) waiver in removal proceedings after the alien has been placed in immigration court proceedings.

Excuses For Criminal Behavior

"He one day approached me and asked if I would marry him for a green card. I of course found the question a bit irregular. I said no at first. He persisted through the course of the month... I have never been very good with saying no. I told him fine. Give me $5000 and a jeep and I will do it."

Stories like this one, reported by the former INS, persuaded Congress to pass the Marriage Fraud Amendments of 1986.

Chapter VI

Marriage Fraud Amendments

Termination of Conditional Status

On November 10, 1986, Congress passed the Immigration Marriage Fraud Amendments of 1986 ("IMFA") to amend the Act in response to allegations by the former INS that marriages for the purpose of obtaining immigration benefits (sham marriages) were rapidly increasing. The reader might recall that EOIR became an independent agency in 1983. The following is a true story about a Special Inquiry Officer in New York who retired long ago. The source of this story is a retired Immigration Judge who was a trial attorney for the former INS in New York before enactment of the IMFA. I'll just call him the trial attorney. A certain case had been scheduled to consider an adjustment application in the New York immigration court. The adjustment application was supported by an approved visa petition filed by a United States citizen. All of the paper work was in order. All parties were present. Nothing was out of the ordinary, except the alien spouse was a woman who was 26 years of age and the United States citizen husband was 74 years of age. When the case was called and the parties announced ready, the Special Inquiry Officer declared without explanation that the case would be reset. The parties appeared about 4 months later, announced ready to proceed, but again the Special Inquiry Officer reset the hearing. The hearing was reset for the third time in a similar fashion. When the respondent and her entourage departed from the courtroom after the third reset, the trial attorney, out of curiosity, asked the Special Inquiry Officer why he kept resetting the hearing when all the papers were in order and both parties had announced ready. The Special Inquiry Officer replied, "You know and I know why she married that guy. And I just want to make sure that he gets his innings in." In the early 1980s baseball was more popular than it seems to be now, making baseball analogies more common. One of the provisions of the IMFA generally utilizes the same technique as the New York Special Inquiry Officer, by imposing a 2 year period of conditional residence on alien spouses who immigrate or adjust to lawful permanent resident status within 2 years of marriage to a United States citizen, as well as their sons and daughters. *See* section 261(g)(1) and (2) of the Act. Pursuant to the IMFA amendments, an alien spouse and his or her United States citizen spouse must submit a petition (Form I-751) for a personal joint interview with a DHS officer 2 years after adjustment to conditional permanent resident status to remove the conditions on the alien spouse's permanent resident status. *See* section 216(c) of the Act. Failure to file the petition or report for the joint interview will result in termination of permanent resident status and will subject the alien spouse to a specially designed removal charge under section 237(a)(1)(D)(i) of the Act. *See* section 216(c)(2) of the Act.

An alien who is subject to removal under section 237(a)(1)(D)(i) of the Act because the DHS terminated the alien's permanent resident status is entitled to discretionary review of the termination decision in removal proceedings before an Immigration Judge. *See* sections 216(b)(2), 216(c)(2)(B), and 216(c)(3)(D) of the Act. After a period of controversy over the nature of review in immigration court, the BIA has determined that review of the termination decision by the DHS *is de novo* (i.e. legalese for a new decision unaffected by a previous decision). *Matter of Herrera Del Orden*, 25 I&N Dec. 589 (BIA 2011) (consideration of any relevant evidence by an Immigration Judge in connection with "review" of a section 216(c)(4) waiver decision

APPROACHING THE BENCH FROM INSIDE THE IMMIGRATION COURT

proper, regardless of whether or not it was previously submitted). Affirmation of *de novo* review policy in immigration court had surfaced earlier in a December 3, 1991 memorandum to the Regional Counsel, Eastern Region, from the former INS Office of the General Counsel. However, the memorandum lacked precedential value and could not be uniformly enforced.

In my opinion, application of the marriage fraud amendments can be confusing, due to the manner in which they were drafted. For example, removal of conditions on permanent resident status is sometimes confused with termination of conditional permanent resident status. Also, the burden of proof sometimes shifts from the alien to the government when the same petition is reviewed in immigration court. Hopefully, the summary that follows will provide a little more clarity.

If the DHS terminates permanent resident status during the first 2 years of the marriage upon finding:

1) the purpose of the marriage was to procure entry to the United States as an immigrant under section 216(b)(1)(A)(i) of the Act;

2) the marriage was annulled or terminated other than through the death of a spouse under section 216(b)(1)(A)(ii) of the Act; or

3) a fee or other consideration (other than attorney's fees) was given for filing the visa petition;

the DHS has the burden in removal proceedings to prove the factual basis for termination by a preponderance of evidence. *See* section 216(b)(2) of the Act. *Matter of Lemhammad*, 20 I&N Dec. 316 (BIA 1991).

If the DHS terminates permanent resident status for failure to file a joint petition to remove the conditions on permanent residence or for failure to attend the required interview under section 216(c)(2)(A) of the Act the respondent must establish compliance in removal proceedings. *See* section 216(c)(2)(B) of the Act.

If the DHS terminates permanent resident status based on an adjudication of the joint petition (after the married couple complies with the joint interview requirements) upon finding that:

1) the qualifying marriage was *not* entered into in accordance with the laws of the place where the marriage took place;
2) the qualifying marriage was judicially annulled or terminated, other than through the death of the spouse;
3) the qualifying marriage was entered into for the purpose of procuring entry as an immigrant; or
4) a fee or other consideration (other than attorney's fees) was given for the filing of a visa petition on behalf of the respondent;

the DHS has the burden of proof to establish the basis of termination by preponderance of evidence in immigration court. *See* section 216(c)(3)(D) of the Act. As a practical matter, this is a reversal of the burden of proof that is applied during the joint interview process where the alien spouse is required to support the petition for removal of conditions on permanent residence with evidence and to rebut any derogatory information that arises during the DHS adjudication. *See* 8 C.F.R. §§ 1216.4(a)(5) and 1216.4(c)(4). Most attorneys realize that shifting the burden of proof might change the ultimate disposition of a contested matter.

For purposes of review in immigration court, an alien must be statutorily eligible for approval of a joint petition to merit review of a DHS denial. *Matter of Tee*, 20 I&N Dec. 949, at 950-51 (BIA 1995). In *Matter of Tee*, the qualifying marriage terminated *after* the former INS denied the joint petition for removal of conditions on permanent residence. The BIA reasoned that the absence of a qualifying marriage warranted statutory denial of the joint petition. *Matter of Tee, supra*, at 951-52. In other words, review of the basis for denial of the joint petition serves no useful purpose in the absence of a qualifying marriage.

APPROACHING THE BENCH FROM INSIDE THE IMMIGRATION COURT

Waiver of Failure to Satisfy Joint Interview Requirements

If an alien cannot qualify for removal of the conditions on permanent residence by satisfying the joint interview requirements of section 216(C)(1) of the Act the alien can apply for a waiver of such requirements by establishing:

1) the alien would experience extreme hardship if removed, limited to the circumstances that existed during the respondent's period of conditional permanent residence (*See* section 216(c)(4)(A) of the Act.); or

2) the alien's good faith marriage terminated, other than by death, and the alien was not at fault in failing to file a timely petition (*See* section 216(c)(4)(B) of the Act.); or

3) the United States citizen or lawful permanent resident spouse battered or perpetuated extreme cruelty on the alien spouse or child. (*See* section 216(c)(4)(C) of the Act.).

The Immigration Judge does not have original jurisdiction over the above described waivers. *Matter of Lemhammad, supra.* However, an Immigration Judge may review the denial of the waivers in removal proceedings. Also, each waiver is independent from the other waivers. Therefore, after the DHS denies one waiver, the respondent cannot seek original consideration of an alternative waiver in immigration court. *Matter of Anderson*, 20 I&N Dec. 888 (BIA 1994). Nevertheless, a respondent is entitled to a reasonable time to file an alternative waiver with the DHS while in immigration court proceedings. *Matter of Mendes*, 20 I&N Dec. 833 (BIA 1994); *Matter of Stowers*, 22 I&N Dec. 605 (BIA 1999). The independent and distinct character of each waiver has led to a counterintuitive (but plain language) interpretation in at least one circuit court that an alien spouse of a United States citizen was not required to prove that her marriage was entered into in good faith to qualify for an extreme hardship waiver under section 216(C)(4)(A) of the Act. *Waggoner v. Gonzales*, 488 F.3d 632 (5th Cir. 2007). Based on this interpretation, an alien could enter into a sham marriage and successfully apply for a hardship waiver if the alien could not satisfy the joint interview requirement upon termination of the marriage within 2 years after adjustment to conditional resident status. This is one example of incongruity in the application of immigration law. It is not the only example.

Governing statute and regulation do not specifically assign the burden of proof for waiver petitions. *See* section 216(c)(4) of the Act; 8 C.F.R. § 1216.5(f). These waivers, however, are forms of relief from removal. Therefore, the respondent should be prepared to carry the burden of proof and persuasion in immigration court proceedings. *See* 8 C.F.R. §§ 1240.11(e) and 1240.8(d). *Matter of Acosta, supra*, at 215-16.

Rescission of Adjustment of Status

Rescission proceedings can result in the revocation of adjustment of status. Therefore, it seems appropriate to address rescission proceedings in juxtaposition to the subject of adjustment of status.

The procedure for rescinding an alien's status begins with a Notice of Intent to Rescind served on the alien by the DHS. The Notice of Intent to Rescind is merely a written notice that can be in letter form. There is no official form. The alien, now referred to as the respondent, has 30 days to file a written answer or request a hearing before an Immigration Judge. If no answer is filed or the notice of intent to rescind is not contested the DHS will rescind the previously granted adjustment of status. *See* 8 C.F.R. §§ 1246.1 and 1246.2. If the DHS rescinds the respondent's status the DHS will issue a final rescission order and rescission proceedings will not take place in immigration court.

If the respondent contests the notice of intent to rescind or requests a hearing before an Immigration Judge the notice of intent to rescind will be forwarded to the immigration court for the conduct of rescission proceedings. *See* 8 C.F.R. § 1246.3. The order of the Immigration Judge in rescission proceedings is limited to termination of rescission proceedings or rescission of adjustment of status. No other form of relief is available. *See* 8 C.F.R. § 1246.6. Rescission proceedings are separate and apart from exclusion, deportation and removal proceedings.

An Immigration Judge shall rescind the action taken to adjust the status of an alien if, within 5 years of such adjustment, it appears that the alien was not in fact eligible for adjustment of status under sections 245, 249, or any other provision of law. *See* section 246(a) of the Act. However, service of the notice of intent to rescind tolls the 5 year period of limitation. *Matter of Pereira*, 19 I&N Dec. 169 (BIA 1984). Rescission of adjustment of status returns the alien to the immigration status he or she had before adjustment of status. *See* section 246(a) of the Act. *Matter of Valiyee*, 14 I&N Dec. 710 (BIA 1974). Therefore, an alien whose status has been rescinded is not necessarily subject to removal, unless he or she had no legal immigration status or is no longer qualified for the immigration status held before the adjustment of status was granted. Thus, if the DHS prevails in rescission proceedings before the Immigration Judge the DHS will ordinarily issue a Notice to Appear to initiate removal proceedings based on the respondent's immigration status that existed before adjustment of status took place.

Burden of Proof

In rescission proceedings, the DHS has the burden to establish by clear, unequivocal and convincing evidence that the alien was ineligible for adjustment of status. *Matter of Vilanova-Gonzalez*, 13 I&N Dec. 399 (BIA 1969). After the enactment of IIRIRA on September 30, 1996, the DHS burden of proof might be interpreted as *clear and convincing* as opposed to *clear, unequivocal and convincing.*

In the absence of fraud or legal dissolution of a marriage at the time of adjustment of status, rescission cannot be solely based on the non-viability of the marriage at the time of the adjustment of status. *Matter of Boromand*, 17 I&N Dec. 450 (BIA 1980); *Matter of Kondo*, 17 I&N Dec. 330 (BIA 1980); *Matter of McKee*, 17 I&N Dec. 332 (BIA 1980).

Adjustment of status based on a labor certification which was subsequently invalidated by the Department of Labor may be rescinded. *Matter of Onal*, 18 I&N Dec. 1981).

Adjustment of status based on an erroneous approval of the foreign residence requirement under section 212(e) of the Act may be rescinded. *Matter of Tayabji*, 19 I&N Dec. 264 (BIA 1981).

Affirmative Defense

An alien may assert eligibility to adjust under a different provision of law at the time of the original adjustment of status as an affirmative defense to rescission. *Matter of Giannoutsos*, 17 I&N Dec. 172 (BIA 1979).

Propriety of Removal Proceedings

As noted above, rescission of adjustment of status is separate and apart from exclusion, deportation and removal proceedings. Therefore, the 5 year limitation for rescission does not bar immigration court proceedings that are based on a ground of inadmissibility (e.g. inadmissible at time of adjustment) that existed prior to or at the time of adjustment of status, even though the 5 year period of limitation has expired. *Matter of S-*, 9 I&N Dec. 548 (BIA 1961; A.G. 1962; BIA 1962); *Matter of Belenzo*, 17 I&N Dec. 374 (BIA 1980, 1981; A.G. 1981).

If the 5 year period of limitation has not expired rescission must be completed before immigration court proceedings can be instituted on a ground that made the alien ineligible for adjustment of status. *Matter of Saunders*, 16 I&N Dec. 326 (BIA 1977).

Currently, the pertinent language of section 237(a)(1)(A) is as follows: "Any alien who at the time of entry *or adjustment of status* was within one or more classes of aliens inadmissible by the law existing at such time is deportable." [Emphasis Added] The current language of section 237(a)(1)(A) of the Act might undermine the holding in *Matter of Saunders, supra.* Section 241(a)(1)(A) of the former Act did not include the phrase "or adjustment of status." It just referred to "time of entry." Nevertheless, at least one appellate court has required rescission of adjustment of status before immigration court proceedings are initiated if the ground for rescission is discovered before the 5 year period of limitation expires. *Garcia v. Attorney General of the United States*, 553 F.3d 724 (3rd Cir. 2009).

On at least one occasion, I have witnessed the termination of permanent resident status by the DHS under section 216 of the Act within 5 years of adjustment of status, based on a perceived defect of the qualifying marriage at time of adjustment. The DHS then initiated removal proceedings based on a charge under section 237(a)(1)(B) of the Act (in the United States in violation of law), instead of section 237(a)(1)(D) of the Act (termination of conditional permanent resident status). In this circumstance, it seems that the DHS must first seek rescission of the adjustment of status before instituting removal proceedings, or charge the respondent under section 237(a)(1)(D) of the Act to allow for review of the termination action in immigration court. Otherwise, the respondent's access to review of the termination of conditional resident status is cut off.

Registry

An alien for whom a record of admission for lawful permanent residence does not exist can apply for registry to create such record under section 249 of the Act. An applicant for registry must satisfy the following conditions:

1) A registry applicant cannot be inadmissible for Nazi persecutions or genocide under section 212(a)(3)(E) of the Act. Nor can a registry applicant be inadmissible as a criminal procurer of prostitution, a prostitute, a person involved in commercialized vice, a subversive, a violator of narcotics laws, or an alien smuggler, under sections 212(a)(2)(A) through (D), 212(a)(3), and 212(a)(6)(E) of the Act.

2) A registry applicant must establish that:

   a. the applicant entered the United States before January 1, 1972;

   b. the applicant has resided continuously in the United States since such entry;

   c. the applicant is a person of good moral character; and

   d. the applicant is not ineligible for United States citizenship, and is not subject to deportation under section 237(a)(4)(B) of the Act (terrorist activities).

Ineligibility for United States citizenship is defined under section 101(a)(19) of the Act (relating to military training and service). *See also* sections 314 and 315 of the Act (deserters and aliens discharged from military service or training based on alienage). However, ineligibility for naturalization based on grounds not described in section 101(a)(19) of the Act cannot be construed as an absolute bar to registry. *See for example Matter of Martin-Arencibia*, 13 I&N Dec. 166 (RC 1969). Martin-Arencibia had been convicted for murder and was ineligible for naturalization, but he was not a draft evader, avoider or deserter. Thus, he was not deemed ineligible for United States citizenship under section 101(a)(19) of the Act.

To establish present status of good moral character, an applicant must show good moral character for a reasonable period of time preceding the filing of the registry application. However, the greater the gravity of the applicant's past misconduct, if any, the longer the period of intervening good conduct must be before the applicant may be able to establish good moral character at the time the application is adjudicated. *Matter of Sanchez-Linn*, 20 I&N Dec. 362 (BIA 1991).

If a waiver of inadmissibility is needed and available to establish eligibility for registry a registry applicant may apply for such waiver in conjunction with his or her registry application. *See* 8 C.F.R. § 1249.1.

An alien may renew an application for registry in immigration court after denial by the DHS. *See* 8 C.F.R. § 1249.2(b).

Once an applicant establishes statutory eligibility for registry, the application may be granted or denied in the exercise of discretion.

Temporary Protected Status

Congress created a form of temporary humanitarian relief to the nationals of designated countries that had suffered natural disasters such as hurricanes and earthquakes in 1990. *See* section 302(a) of the Immigration Act of 1990 ("IMMACT 1990"). However, experience has taught all of us who have worked in the immigration arena that there is nothing more permanent than a temporary resident. The provisions for temporary protected status ("TPS") are now found under section 244 of the Act.

To be eligible for TPS under section 244 of the Act, an applicant must prove that he or she:

1) is a national of a state designated under section 244(b)(1) of the Act (or in the case of an alien having no nationality is a person who last habitually resided in a designated state);

2) has been continuously physically present in the United States since the effective date of the most recent designation of the state;

3) has continuously resided in the United States since any date identified by the Attorney General for purposes of temporary protected status;

4) is admissible as an immigrant, except exclusion grounds under sections 212(a)(5) (aliens required to have a labor certification) and 212(a)(7)(A) (aliens required to have an immigrant visa) do not apply; and

5) has registered for temporary protected status during a registration period of not less than 180 days.

An alien who has been convicted for a felony, or two or more misdemeanors committed in the United States is not eligible for TPS. *See* section 244(c)(2)(B)(i) of the Act. Likewise, an alien described in section 208(b)(2)(A) of the Act is not eligible for TPS. Aliens described in section 208(b)(2)(A) of the Act are aliens who have participated in persecution, have been convicted of a particularly serious crime, or there are serious reasons to believe the alien has committed a serious nonpolitical crime outside the United States prior to arrival in the United States. The disqualifying criteria described in section 208(b)(2)(A) of the Act are discussed in Chapter III in the context of persecution claims.

No waiver is available to a TPS applicant who is subject to exclusion under sections 212(a)(2)(A) or 212(a)(2)(B) of the Act (relating to criminals); section 212(a)(2)(C) of the Act (relating to drug offenses), except for a single offense of simple possession of 30 grams or less of marihuana; and sections 212(a)(3)(A), (B), (C), and (E) of the Act (relating to national security, Nazi persecutions, and participation in genocide).

Physical presence is not cut off by brief, casual and innocent absences from the United States. *See* section 244(c)(4)(A) and (B) of the Act.

There is a tendency among some immigration attorneys to

APPROACHING THE BENCH FROM INSIDE THE IMMIGRATION COURT

treat TPS like other forms of relief from removal. In fact, a grant of TPS does not prevent the DHS from pursuing a removal order, even if such order cannot be executed as long as the alien enjoys TPS status. Therefore, it is not proper for an Immigration Judge to terminate removal proceedings based on a grant of TPS. *Matter of Sosa-Ventura*, 25 I&N Dec. 391 (BIA 2010). For example, if a respondent qualifies for TPS in immigration court proceedings and no other relief from removal is available the Immigration Judge will ordinarily grant TPS and issue a removal order. In this circumstance, however, there might be a possibility of administration closure (an indefinite postponement) which simply removes the case from the active docket. For this same reason, it may be difficult to justify a motion to reopen removal proceedings to allow consideration of a TPS application. Even if removal proceedings are reopened, a grant of TPS will not alter the previous disposition of the case.

Finally, in spite of some blurry TPS regulations under 8 C.F.R. Part 1244 that are subject to various interpretations an alien has a right to apply for TPS in removal proceedings, even if the alien's application had previously been denied by the DHS Administrative Appeals Unit. *See* section 244(b)(5)(B) of the Act. *Matter of Barrientos*, 24 I&N Dec. 100 (BIA 2007).

Chapter VII

Waivers

Immigrant Document Waivers

The familiar "green card" (Form I-551) issued to lawful permanent residents of the United States is valid as a travel document *if* the card holder has not been absent from the United States for 1 year or more. *See* 8 C.F.R. § 211.1(a)(2). Other travel documents are deemed acceptable for returning lawful permanent residents. *See* 8 C.F.R. § 211.1(a)(1) through (7).

An immigrant alien returning from a temporary visit abroad to an unrelinquished residence in the United States, who is without a valid immigrant visa or travel document, can apply for a waiver under section 211(b) of the Act. *See* 8 C.F.R. § 1211.4(a). The DHS makes the initial decision which can be renewed without prejudice in immigration court. *See* 8 C.F.R. § 1211.4(b). To be eligible for this waiver, the applicant cannot be otherwise inadmissible or subject to removal. An otherwise inadmissible alien who qualifies for an exception under section 237(a)(1)(H) of the Act remains eligible to apply for a section 211(b) document waiver. Section 237(a)(1)(H) of the Act is a waiver provision for aliens who are inadmissible under section 237(a)(1)(A) of the Act (inadmissible at time of entry) in conjunction with section 212(a)(6)(C)(i) of the Act (fraud or willful misrepresentation of a material fact). This waiver will be discussed in more detail immediately following this discussion of the immigrant document waiver.

Once an applicant establishes statutory eligibility for a waiver under section 211(b) of the Act, the waiver may be granted or denied in the exercise of discretion.

It is not unusual for the DHS to assert that a returning lawful permanent resident who has been absent for 1 year or more from the United States has abandoned his or her permanent resident status. This assertion obviously adds another dimension to an otherwise simple waiver application. The abandonment issue must be addressed first before the waiver under section 211(b) can be considered. One of the leading BIA decisions relating to abandonment of permanent residence is *Matter of Huang*, 19 I&N Dec. 749 (BIA 1988). The BIA held in *Matter of Huang* that:

> Where an applicant for admission to the United States has a colorable claim to returning resident status, the burden is on the Immigration and Naturalization Service to show by clear, unequivocal, and convincing evidence that the applicant should be deprived of his or her lawful permanent residence.

After enactment of IIRIRA on September 30, 1996, the applicable burden of proof for the DHS might convert from "clear, unequivocal, and convincing" evidence to "clear and convincing" evidence. This conversion would be consistent with the burden of proof imposed on the DHS to establish a removal charge. *See* 8 C.F.R. § 1240.8(a).

Waiver Under Section 237(a)(1)(H) of the Act

A waiver under section 237(a)(1)(H) of the Act is available for aliens who are deportable under section 237(a)(1)(A) of the Act (inadmissible at time of admission) based on fraud or misrepresentation at the time of admission to the United States under section 212(a)(6)(C)

(i) of the Act (fraud or willful misrepresentation of a material fact). Congress provided this waiver to prevent the breakup of families. *See INS v. Errico*, 385 U.S. 214 (1966).

An applicant for the 237(a)(1)(H) waiver must establish:

1) the applicant is a spouse, parent, son or daughter of a United States citizen or lawful permanent resident; and

2) was in possession of an immigrant visa or equivalent document; and

3) was otherwise admissible at the time of entry, except for lack of a labor certificate under section 212(a)(5)(A) of the Act or lack of a proper immigrant document under section 212(a)(7)(A) of the Act which was a direct result of the fraud or misrepresentation. *Matter of Roman*, 19 I&N Dec. 855 (BIA 1988); or

4) the applicant is an abused spouse who is a self-petitioner.

A waiver under section 237(a)(1)(H) of the Act will waive deportation based on any ground of inadmissibility arising from the fraud or misrepresentation that occurred at the time of admission. *Matter of Anabo*, 18 I&N Dec. 87 (BIA 1981). Even where the DHS does not allege fraud, the BIA has held that a waiver under section 237(a)(1)(H) can be applied to waive inadmissibility under section 212(a)(7)(A)(i)(I) for lack of a valid immigrant visa or entry document. *Matter of Fu*, 23 I&N Dec. 985 (BIA 2006). In *Matter of Fu*, the respondent became ineligible for his immigrant visa due to the demise of his father (the visa petitioner) before the respondent was admitted with the immigrant visa.

A waiver under section 237(a)(1)(H) of the Act is *not* available:

1) to waive fraud committed to procure adjustment of status. *Matter of Connelly*, 19 I&N Dec. 156 (BIA 1984);

2) to waive inadmissibility arising from a fraudulent marriage. *Matter of Matti*, 19 I&N Dec. 43 (BIA 1984);

3) to waive a removal ground based on Nazi persecution described under section 237(a)(4)(D) of the Act;

4) in rescission proceedings. *Matter of Pereira,* 19 I&N Dec. 169 (BIA 1984).

Once an applicant establishes statutory eligibility for this waiver, the waiver application may be granted or denied in the exercise of discretion. *See Matter of Tijam,* 22 I&N Dec. 408, 412-14 (BIA 1998).

Waiver of Unlawful Presence

Generally, unlawful presence in the United States is the presence in the United States of nonimmigrant aliens who have remained longer than permitted and aliens who are present in the United States without admission or parole (i.e. aliens who have entered the United States without inspection). The term, "unlawful presence," does not apply to lawful permanent residents. *See* section 212(a)(9)(B)(ii) of the Act.

An alien (other than a lawful permanent resident) who was unlawfully present in the United States for more than 180 days, but less than 1 year, and departs from the United States is inadmissible to the United States if such alien applies for admission within 3 years of the alien's departure. Likewise, an alien who was unlawfully present in the United States for 1 year or more, and who seeks admission to the United States within 10 years of the alien's departure date is inadmissible. *See* section 212(a)(9)(B)(i) of the Act.

An immigrant alien who is not admissible to the United States under section 212(a)(9)(B)(i) of the Act because of unlawful presence may apply for a discretionary waiver under section 212(a)(9)(B)(v) of the Act. To establish threshold eligibility for this waiver, the applicant must establish that:

1) the applicant is the spouse, son, or daughter of a United States citizen or lawful permanent resident of the United States; and

2) refusal of admission would result in extreme hardship to the

APPROACHING THE BENCH FROM INSIDE THE IMMIGRATION COURT

United States citizen or lawful permanent resident spouse or parent.

An alien who has been unlawfully present in the United States for an aggregate period of more than 1 year or had been ordered removed from the United States and who enters or attempts to enter the United States without inspection is inadmissible to the United States. *See* section 212(a)(9)(C)(i) of the Act.

The waiver for the ground of inadmissibility under section 212(a)(9)(C)(i) of the Act is only available to self-petitioning battered spouses or children. *See* section 212(a)(9)(C)(iii) of the Act. Except for battered spouses and children, no waiver is available for section 212(a)(9)(C)(i) of the Act. *Matter of Torres-Garcia*, 23 I&N Dec. 866 (BIA 2006).

Congress provided only one exception to inadmissibility under section 212(a)(9)(C)(i) of the Act. The exception applies if an alien seeks admission more than 10 years after the alien's last departure from the United States and the Secretary of Homeland Security has consented to the alien's reapplication for admission prior to the alien's embarkation from a foreign place or application for admission from a contiguous foreign territory. The same exception applies to aliens who are inadmissible under section 212(a)(9)(A). These are arriving aliens who are seeking admission to the United States within 5 years after removal and arriving aliens who are seeking admission to the United States within 10 years of an order of removal, or within 20 years of removal or an order of removal in the case of aliens convicted of an aggravated felony defined under section 101(a)(43) of the Act). *See* section 212(a)(9)(A)(iii) of the Act.

An Immigration Judge may grant permission to reapply for admission to the United States retroactively (i.e. *nunc pro tunc*, legalese meaning "now for then") even if such permission was denied by the DHS. *See Matter of Ng*, 17 I&N Dec. 63 (BIA 1979). However, an Immigration Judge may not grant *nunc pro tunc* permission to reapply for admission to the United States if other grounds of inadmissibility exist. *See Matter of Ng, supra; Matter of Garcia-Linares*, 21 I&N Dec. 254 (BIA 1996). In other words, if any other ground of inadmissibility would remain after granting permission to reapply for admission to the United States an Immigration Judge cannot grant such permission *nunc pro tunc.*

It is interesting to note that using the date of departure to define the time period that an alien must wait to apply for admission to the United States after any period of unlawful presence seems to encourage aliens to remain in the United States unlawfully. As soon as an alien departs the alien becomes inadmissible under section 212(a)(9)(B) of the Act, but if the alien does not depart and remains unlawfully present in the United States the alien is not inadmissible under section 212(a)(9)(B) of the Act. For example, an alien who has remained longer than permitted after admission as a nonimmigrant and is the beneficiary of an immediate relative visa petition will be eligible for adjustment of status under section 245 of the Act so long as the alien remains unlawfully present in the United States. If the same alien departs from the United States and returns (even if the alien is inspected and admitted) before adjusting status to lawful permanent residence the alien is inadmissible and, therefore, ineligible for adjustment to lawful permanent resident status for 3 or 10 years after departure.

Waiver Under Section 212(c) of the Former Act

One of my colleagues during my days on the bench simply described section 212(c) of the former Act as the "forgiveness statute." Awareness of more than 40 years of legal wrangling over the application of section 212(c) of the Act and its ultimate repeal under section 304(b) of IIRIRA in 1996 caused me to tacitly question the competence of my colleague for such a gross oversimplification. Further reflection, however, ultimately convinced me that describing section 212(c) of the former Act as a forgiveness statute is basically accurate. Setting aside the complex specious legal rationales for applying an exclusion waiver in deportation proceedings and legal hoops through which

Excuses For Criminal Behavior

"I pled guilty because I might have got 99 years if the judge knew the truth."

The expressed motive for this guilty plea does not suggest reliance on a potential 212(c) waiver. Nevertheless, the un-rebuttable presumption of reliance established in *United States v. St. Cyr*, 533 U.S. 289 (2001) applies so long as the alien would have been eligible for 212(c) relief at the time of the plea under the law then in effect.

one must leap to avoid technical disqualification, the subsequent adjudication simply amounts to weighing the favorable factors against adverse factors to determine in a pure exercise of discretion whether the alien should be allowed to keep his or her permanent residence in the United States. This approximates forgiveness of past misconduct.

Section 212(c) of the former Act, although it has been repealed, still applies to some lawful permanent resident aliens due to a United States Supreme Court decision. Specifically, the United States Supreme Court held that "212(c) relief remains available for aliens. . .whose convictions were obtained through plea agreements and who. . .would have been eligible for 212(c) relief at the time of their plea under the law then in effect." *United States v. St. Cyr*, 533 U.S. 289 (2001). So, in spite of the repeal of section 212(c) of the former Act on September 30, 1996, 212(c) relief remains available for some permanent resident aliens whose criminal trials took place before the repeal of the waiver. *See* section 304(b) of IIRIRA (repealing section 212(c) of the former Act).

Section 212(c) of the Act provides that aliens lawfully admitted for permanent residence who temporarily proceed abroad voluntarily (not under a deportation order) and are returning to a lawful unrelinquished domicile of at least 7 consecutive years may be admitted in the discretion of the Attorney General regardless of certain exclusion grounds. However, a lawful permanent resident remains eligible to apply for a 212(c) waiver, even though he or she is *not* returning from a trip abroad. *Matter of Silva*, 16 I&N Dec. 26 (BIA 1976); *Francis v. INS*, 532 F.2d 268 (2nd Cir. 1976). This appears to be an example of judges and bureaucrats rewriting a statute by deleting the requirement of returning from abroad to an unrelinquished domicile in the United States to qualify for a 212(c) waiver.

Section 212(c) of the Act does not provide an indiscriminate waiver for any applicant who establishes statutory eligibility for such relief. Instead, an applicant must demonstrate that his or her application merits the favorable exercise of discretion. *Matter of*

Excuses For Criminal Behavior

Q: Please explain the circumstances of your arrest for aggravated robbery.

A: Well, I was walking down the road, minding my own business, when a car drove by and someone threw something at me out of the car. I made a sign with my hands and the car suddenly turned around and they started shooting at me. I began running down the road for my life, and I had a blade in my hand. When I ran into a Kentucky Fried Chicken, the people all got scared and ran out, and one of them called the police.

Q: What happened at your criminal trial?

A: I pleaded "guilty."

The precise motivation behind this respondent's guilty plea remains undisclosed, but he nevertheless is the beneficiary of the *United States v. St. Cyr* presumption of reliance on a potential 212(c) waiver.

Buscemi, 19 I&N Dec. 628 (BIA 1988); *Matter of Marin*, 16 I&N Dec. 581 (BIA 1978). This exercise of discretion involves the balancing of favorable social and humane considerations against the adverse factors indicating undesirability as a lawful permanent resident of the United States.

Favorable factors have been found to include:

1) family ties in the United States;
2) residence of long duration, especially when the residence began at a young age (including temporary residence acquired under sections 245A or 210 of the Act), 8 C.F.R. § 1212.3(f)(2), *White v. INS*, 75 F.3d 213 (5th Cir. 1996);
3) the hardship of deportation or removal on the respondent and his or her family;
4) service in the armed forces of the United States;
5) a steady employment history;
6) property and business ties in the United States;
7) value and service to the community;
8) genuine rehabilitation in the presence of a criminal history (rehabilitation not an absolute requirement to a favorable exercise of discretion, *Matter of Edwards*, 20 I&N Dec. 191 (BIA 1990)); and
9) evidence of good character.

Adverse factors have been found to be:

1) the nature and circumstances of the exclusion ground relating to the applicant;
2) significant violations of immigration laws of the United States;
3) the nature, recency, and seriousness of the criminal record if it exists; and
4) evidence of bad character

See Matter of Marin, supra.

It is important to note that the weight of the applicant's burden

APPROACHING THE BENCH FROM INSIDE THE IMMIGRATION COURT

to produce offsetting equities to meet threshold eligibility for a 212(c) waiver increases as negative factors grow more serious. This burden to offset negative factors could increase to a point where "unusual or outstanding equities" are required. This is likely to occur when a serious single crime or a pattern of criminal activity exists. However, a showing of "unusual or outstanding equities" is not a condition precedent to the balancing of favorable and adverse factors. *Matter of Sotelo*, 23 I&N Dec. 201 (BIA 2001).

An Immigration Judge must deny an application for a 212(c) waiver if:

1) the applicant is not a lawful permanent resident;
2) the applicant has not maintained a lawful domicile in the United States as lawful permanent resident (or temporary resident under sections 245A or 210 of the Act (1986 amnesty provisions)) immediately preceding the filing of the waiver application, *Matter of Ponce De Leon-Ruiz*, 21 I&N Dec. 154 (BIA 1996, A.G. 1997, BIA 1997);
3) the applicant is inadmissible for security related grounds Under sections 212(a)(3)(A), (B), (C), or (E) of the Act; or
4) the applicant has been charged and found to be subject to deportation or removal based on a conviction for an aggravated felony as defined under section 101(a)(43) of the Act (at the time the application is adjudicated), *except* for applicants whose plea agreements (under the rationale in *United States v. St. Cyr, supra*) took place on or after November 29, 1990, but before April 24, 1996 (the effective date of the Antiterrorism and Effective Death Penalty Act of 1996 ("AEDPA")), *and who have not* served a term of imprisonment of at least 5 years or more for the aggravated felony or felonies; and *except* for aliens whose aggravated felony conviction is based on a plea agreement that occurred before November 29, 1990. *See* section 501(b) of the Immigration Act of 1990 (where Congress provided a time limit for application of the

aggravated felony definition relating to certain offenses). *Matter of A-A-*, 20 I&N Dec. 492 (BIA 1992).

See 8 C.F.R. § 1212.3(f).

I have not included the disabling provision under 8 C.F.R. § 1212.3(f)(5) (no statutory counterpart in section in section 212 of the Act for aliens subject to deportation or removal under section 241 of the former Act or 237 of the Act) because the United States Supreme Court has disapproved the comparable ground or statutory counterpart rationale. *Judulang v. Holder*, 132 S. Ct. 476 (2011). The comparable ground or statutory counterpart rationale involves a comparison of a deportation ground (241 of the former Act or 237 of the Act) under which an applicant for a 212(c) waiver is found to be deportable or removable to grounds of inadmissibility under section 212 of the Act. If an applicant can find a matching ground of inadmissibility (e.g. conviction for distribution of a controlled substance) the applicant is eligible to apply for the waiver. However, if a matching ground cannot be found (e.g. conviction for possession of a firearm) the applicant is not eligible to apply for a 212(c) waiver.

The following is a 212(c) waiver worksheet that can be used to prepare for a hearing relating to a 212(c) waiver in immigration court:

APPROACHING THE BENCH FROM INSIDE THE IMMIGRATION COURT

212(c)/Cancellation of Removal Worksheet

I. Duration of Lawful Permanent Residence[1]:

II. Age at inception of LPR status:

III. Family Ties:[2]
    United States:

    Foreign:

IV. Hardship
    Respondent:

    Family:

V. Property and Business Ties:

VI. Value and Service to Community

---

1   *Matter of Buscemi*, 19 I&N Dec. 628 (BIA 1988): Respondent had 17 years of lawful permanent resident status beginning at 9 years of age; *Matter of Arreguin*, 21 I&N Dec. 38 (BIA 1995): Respondent had 20 years of lawful permanent resident status beginning at 22 years of age. Outstanding equities were found.

2   *Matter of Arreguin, supra*: Minor children who were 3 and 11 years of age found to be an outstanding equity.

WILLIAM K. ZIMMER

VII. Service in the Armed Forces of the United States

VIII. Criminal Offenses
Nature, Recency and Seriousness:

	Offense	Commission Date	Conviction Date	Dispostion/ Sentence
1)				
2)				
3)				
4)				
5)				

IX. Rehabilitation (not absolute requirement, *Matter of Edwards*, 20 I&N Dec. 191 (BIA 1990)):

X. Character:

Excuses For Criminal Behavior

"I don't have a drinking problem because I never drink enough to forget everything."

The author of this excuse seems to have discovered an elegant test for identifying a drinking problem. Rehabilitation is not an absolute requirement to qualify for a 212(c) waiver or cancellation of removal for lawful permanent residents. *Matter of Edwards*, 20 I&N Dec. 191 (BIA 1990).

Cancellation of Removal For Lawful Permanent Residents

Section 240A(a) of the Act provides that the Attorney General of the United States may cancel the removal from the United States of a lawful permanent resident who is inadmissible or deportable if the applicant for relief:

1) has held lawful permanent resident status for at least 5 years;

2) has resided in the United States continuously for 7 years after admission in any status, (*Matter of Blancas-Lara*, 23 I&N Dec. 458 (BIA 2002); and

3) has not been convicted for an aggravated felony defined under section 101(a)(43) of the Act.

Once an applicant has established statutory eligibility for cancellation of removal, relief may be granted or denied in the exercise of discretion. General standards developed in *Matter of Marin, supra*, at 584-85, for the exercise of discretion under section 212(c) of the former Act, are applicable to the exercise of discretion for cancellation of removal applications. *Matter of C-V-T-*, 22 I&N Dec. 7 (BIA 1998).

Continuous Residence

Section 240A(d) of the Act provides that continuous residence of a lawful permanent resident who is applying for cancellation of removal ends under the following circumstances:

1) when the DHS serves a Notice to Appear or Order to Show Cause, (*See* section 309(c)(5) of IIRIRA as amended by section 203(a) of NACARA; *Matter of Nolasco*, 22 I&N Dec. 632 (BIA 1999)); or

2) when the applicant commits a crime classified under section 212(a)(2) of the Act that renders the applicant inadmissible

under section 212(a)(2) of the Act or removable under section 237(a)(2) and/or section 237(a)(4) of the Act. *Matter of Perez*, 22 I&N Dec. 689 (BIA 1999).

The earliest occurrence of either circumstance ends continuous residence.

Aliens Ineligible For Cancellation of Removal

The following aliens are not eligible for relief under section 240A(a) of the Act:

1) aliens who entered the United States as a crewman subsequent to June 30, 1964;
2) aliens who were admitted as or became exchange visitors under section 101(a)(15)(J) of the Act in order to receive a graduate medical degree or training;
3) aliens who were admitted or became exchange visitors under section 101(a)(15)(J) of the Act other than to receive a graduate medical degree or training, and are subject to the 2 year foreign residency requirement without having obtained a waiver or fulfilled the requirement;
4) aliens who are inadmissible under section 212(a)(3) of the Act or deportable under section 237(a)(4) of the Act (security or terrorist grounds);
5) aliens who participated in the persecution of others within the meaning of section 241(b)(3)(B)(i) of the Act; and
6) aliens who have been granted cancellation of removal, suspension of deportation under section 244 of the former Act, or a waiver under section 212(c) of the former Act.

General Nonimmigrant Waiver

A bona fide nonimmigrant (e.g. an alien having a foreign residence which the alien has no intention of abandoning and is visiting the United States temporarily) who is not inadmissible as:

1) a security risk under section 212(a)(3)(A) of the Act (except for violators of laws governing the export of technology and sensitive information, under section 212(a)(3)(A)(i)(II) of the Act);
2) a foreign policy concern under section 212(a)(3)(C) of the Act; or
3) a Nazi persecutor under section 212(a)(3)(E) of the Act;

can apply for a waiver of ineligibility for a nonimmigrant visa under section 212(d)(3)(B) of the Act. However, an applicant must first apply to the DHS. If the application is not submitted prior to arrival (i.e. to a United States consular officer) the applicant must establish that the ground for inadmissibility that requires a waiver could not have been discovered through the exercise of reasonable diligence. *See* 8 C.F.R. § 1212.4(b).

This waiver application may be renewed before an Immigration Judge upon denial by DHS. *See* 8 C.F.R. § 1212.4(b).

Once an applicant has established statutory eligibility for a 212(d)(3)(b) waiver, the application may be granted or denied in the exercise of discretion. The exercise of discretion requires consideration of at least 3 factors:

1) the risk of harm to society if the applicant is admitted;
2) the seriousness of the applicant's immigration law or criminal law violation(s) if any; and
3) the nature of the applicant's reasons for wishing to enter the United States.

See Matter of Hranka, 16 I&N Dec. 491 (BIA 1978). The BIA held in *Matter of Hranka*, that, although the applicant had been deported for engaging in prostitution, rehabilitation and the presence of close

APPROACHING THE BENCH FROM INSIDE THE IMMIGRATION COURT

relatives living across the border in the United States justified the grant of a waiver.

Unlike the 212(c) waiver, a waiver under section 212(d)(3)(B) of the Act may not be granted *nunc pro tunc* (legalese meaning "now for then") in immigration court proceedings. *Matter of Fueyo*, 20 I&N Dec. 84 (BIA 1984). In *Matter of Fueyo*, the applicant was subject to a deportation charge as opposed to a charge of inadmissibility. In other words, the applicant had been found in the United States after a previous entry and was not applying for admission to the United States. The 212(d)(3)(B) waiver is a waiver of inadmissibility: It does not waive a deportation ground.

Nonimmigrant Document Waiver

A bona fide nonimmigrant (e.g. an alien having a foreign residence which the alien has no intention of abandoning and is visiting the United States temporarily) who is without a valid passport and/or nonimmigrant visa as required under section 212(a)(7)(B)(i) of the Act can apply for a waiver under section 212(d)(4) of the Act. The language of the statute requires State Department concurrence. However, effective on January 11, 1994, the United States State Department authorized district directors of the former INS to grant or deny these waivers without its concurrence. Immigration Judges do not have this authority. *See* 22 C.F.R. § 41.2(j) and 59 F.R. 1473 (1-11-94).

An applicant for a 212(d)(4) waiver must qualify under at least one of three conditions:

1) an unforeseen emergency in individual cases;
2) reciprocity between sovereign states of contiguous territories or adjacent islands of which the applicant is a national; or
3) the applicant is proceeding in immediate and continuous transit through the United States under a contract authorized

under section 233(c) of the Act (contracts between the United States and commercial carriers).

Smuggling Waivers
Inadmissible Aliens

A waiver under section 212(d)(11) of the Act is available to certain aliens who are inadmissible under section 212(a)(6)(E) of the Act for alien smuggling. An applicant for this waiver must establish that:

1) the applicant is a lawful permanent resident of the United States who voluntarily and temporarily proceeded abroad and is otherwise admissible to the United States *or* an alien who is seeking admission or adjustment of status as a spouse, parent, son, or daughter of a United States citizen or lawful permanent resident of the United States; and

2) the applicant is inadmissible for smuggling *only* a spouse, parent, son, or daughter, *and no other individual*, into the United States. *Matter of Compean*, 21 I&N Dec. 51 (BIA 1995).

The 212(d)(11) waiver is not available if the smuggling activity preceded the formation of the required familial relationship. *Matter of Farias Mendoza*, 21 I&N Dec. 269 (BIA 1996; A.G. 1997; BIA 1997). For example, a lawful permanent resident of the United States who smuggles a fiancé into the United States and marries him or her after the smuggling transaction took place is not eligible for the waiver, even if the marriage takes place before the waiver application is filed.

Excuses For Criminal Behavior

"I was convicted for transporting undocumented aliens because I had fourteen people, and needed to sell them for Christmas money."

It is important to distinguish between transporting and smuggling. Congress proscribed transporting and harboring aliens with knowledge or in reckless disregard of such aliens' unlawful entry into the United States in furtherance of the violation of law in a separate section from the section prohibiting unlawful entry. *See* sections 274 and 275 of the Act, respectively. The U.S. Attorney's Office usually charges alien smuggling under 18 U.S.C. § 2 in conjunction with section 275 of the Act (i.e. aiding, abetting, inducing an alien to enter the United States in violation of law). *See Martinez-Serrano*, 25 I&N Dec. 151 (BIA 2009).

Deportable Aliens

A waiver under section 237(a)(1)(E)(iii) of the Act is available to certain aliens who are deportable under section 237(a)(1)(E)(i) of the Act for alien smuggling. An applicant for this waiver must establish that:

1) the applicant is a lawful permanent resident of the United States; and
2) the applicant is deportable for smuggling *only* a spouse, parent, son, or daughter, *and no other individual.*

Once an applicant establishes statutory eligibility for any of the smuggling waivers, the waiver application may be granted or denied in the exercise of discretion.

It is important to note that an alien is not inadmissible or deportable under sections 212(a)(6)(E)(i) or 237(a)(1)(E) of the Act if the alien:

1) is an eligible immigrant under the family unity provisions of section 301(b)(1) of the Immigration Act of 1990;
2) was physically present in the United States on May 5, 1988;
3) is seeking admission as a spouse or unmarried son or daughter of a lawful permanent resident of the United States;
4) engaged in the smuggling activity for which he or she is inadmissible before May 5, 1988; and
5) the smuggling activity involved *only* a spouse, parent, son, or daughter, *and no other individual.*

Waiver For Aliens Subject to Civil Penalty For Document Fraud

Section 274C of the Act generally prohibits counterfeiting or altering documents, or possessing, or using fraudulent documents. Section 274C also provides for cease and desist orders and civil money penalties for prohibited activities. Congress established a ground of inadmissibility for any alien who is the subject of a final order for

Excuses For Criminal Behavior

"I agreed to help my friend smuggle her cousin into the United States because I was angry with my husband and I needed the money to take my kids to SeaWorld."

The friend's cousin is not a *spouse, parent, son, or daughter*. Therefore, the author of this excuse is not eligible for a waiver under section 212(d)(11) or section 237(a)(1)(E)(iii) of the Act.

violation of section 274C of the Act. *See* section 212(a)(6)(F)(i) of the Act. Congress also provided for a discretionary waiver of section 212(a)(6)(F)(i) of the Act. *See* sections 212(a)(6)(F)(ii) and 212(d)(12) of the Act.

To qualify for a waiver under section 212(d)(12) of the Act, an applicant must establish that:

1) the applicant is a lawful permanent resident of the United States;
2) the applicant temporarily proceeded abroad (not under an order of deportation or removal); and
3) the applicant is otherwise admissible; or
4) the applicant is seeking admission or adjustment of status as an immediate relative under section 201(b)(2)(A) of the Act or as a family sponsored immigrant under section 203(a) of the Act.

This waiver is not available if more than one civil money penalty had been imposed against the applicant under section 274C of the Act and if the offense was committed to benefit an individual other than the applicant's spouse or child.

During my tenure on the immigration bench, I have never had occasion to consider a 212(d)(12) waiver.

Waiver For Victims of Domestic Violence

On September 30, 1996, Congress added a deportation ground that applies to aliens convicted of crimes of domestic violence, stalking, child abuse and violations of protective orders. *See* section 350 of the IIRIRA, adding section 237(a)(2)(E) of the Act. On October 28, 2000, Congress added section 237(a)(7) of the Act to provide a waiver of section 237(a)(2)(E) of the Act for aliens convicted of crimes of domestic violence, stalking, child abuse and violations of protective orders, who have been battered or subjected to extreme cruelty. *See* section 1505(b)(1), title V of the Battered Immigrant Women Protection Act of 2001.

To be eligible for a waiver for victims of domestic violence under section 237(a)(7) of the Act, an applicant must demonstrate:

1) battery or subjection to extreme cruelty; and
2) the applicant is not and was not the primary perpetrator of violence in the domestic relationship.

Next a determination must be made that:

1) the applicant was acting in self defense; or
2) the applicant had violated a protection order intended to protect the applicant; or
3) the applicant's violation:
   a. did not result in serious bodily injury; and
   b. there was a connection between the alien's violation and the battery or extreme cruelty suffered by the applicant.

The Immigration Judge is authorized to consider any credible and relevant evidence in making a determination regarding a 237(a)(7) waiver.

I have never had an opportunity to consider a 237(a)(7) waiver during my tenure as an Immigration Judge.

Waiver Under Section 212(h) of the Act

A waiver of inadmissibility under section 212(h) of the Act is limited to the waiver of subparagraphs 212(a)(2)(A)(i)(I), (B), (D), and (E), and subparagraph 212(a)(2)(A)(i)(II) of the Act. These categories of inadmissible aliens include:

1) aliens who are convicted of or admit the commission of a crime or crimes involving moral turpitude (section 212(a)(2)(A)(i)(I) of the Act);

2) aliens convicted of multiple crimes for which the aggregate sentences amount to 5 years or more, whether or not they involve moral turpitude (section 212(a)(2)(B) of the Act);
3) aliens involved in prostitution or commercialized vice (section 212(a)(2)(D) of the Act);
4) aliens involved in serious criminal activity who have asserted immunity from prosecution (section 212(a)(2)(E) of the Act); and
5) aliens who are convicted of or admit the commission of a *single offense* of simple possession of marihuana weighing 30 grams or less (section 212(a)(2)(A)(i)(II) of the Act).

The term "serious criminal activity" means:

1) any felony;
2) any crime of violence, as defined in 18 U.S.C. § 16; or
3) any crime of reckless driving or of driving while intoxicated if such crime involves personal injury to another person.

See section 101(h) of the Act.

An applicant for a 212(h) waiver must qualify under one of three sets of criteria. The first set of criteria under section 212(h)(1)(A) of the Act requires proof that:

1) the applicant is inadmissible only for prostitution or procurement of prostitutes or proceeds from prostitution under section 212(a)(2)(D)(i) or (ii) of the Act (i.e. not inadmissible for coming to the United States to engage in commercialized vice, whether or not related to prostitution, under section 212(a)(2)(D)(iii) of the Act); or
2) the activities for which the applicant is inadmissible occurred more than 15 years before the application for a visa, admission, or adjustment of status; and
3) the applicant's admission to the United States would not be contrary to the national welfare, safety, or security of the United States; and

Excuses For Criminal Behavior

Q: Please explain why you were convicted for possession of cocaine.

A: I was using cocaine because I was depressed.

Q: Why were you depressed?

A: Because I was living with my mother-in-law.

The 212(h) waiver is a limited waiver. It can only be used to waive removal grounds based on controlled substance offenses that involve a single offense of simple possession of *marihuana* weighing 30 grams or less (regardless of the presence of mitigating discretionary factors). Therefore, the author of this excuse is not eligible for a waiver under section 212(h) of the Act.

4) the applicant has been rehabilitated.

The second alternative set of criteria under section 212(h)(1)(B) of the Act requires proof that:

1) the applicant is the spouse, parent, son, or daughter of a United States citizen or lawful permanent resident of the United States; and

2) the applicant's exclusion would result in extreme hardship to one or more of the above described qualifying relatives.

It is important to note that the qualifying relatives for a 212(h) waiver differ from the qualifying relatives recognized for suspension of deportation and cancellation of removal for non-permanent residents. The reader will recall that only hardship to a United States citizen or lawful permanent resident spouse, parent or *child* can be considered for suspension of deportation and cancellation of removal applicants. A child cannot be 21 years of age or older. *See* section 101(b)(1) of the Act. A *son or daughter* can be a person who is 21 years of age or older. Thus, the pool of qualifying relatives for a 212(h) waiver applicant is deeper than the pool of qualifying relatives for a suspension of deportation or cancellation of removal applicant.

The third alternative set of criteria under section 212(h)(1)(C) of the Act only requires proof that the applicant is a battered spouse or child.

For all three alternatives, the Attorney General must consent to an application or re-application for a visa, admission to the United States, or adjustment of status. This consent is discretionary and is dictated to a great extent by statute and regulation. *See* section 212(h)(2) of the Act; 8 C.F.R. § 1212.7(d).

In practice, most applicants are limited by surrounding circumstances to applications under the second alternative set of criteria that requires proof of extreme hardship to one or more qualifying relatives. *See* section 212(h)(1)(B) of the Act.

Extreme Hardship

Extreme hardship for the purpose of a 212(h) waiver application is analogous to the same term used in the context of suspension of deportation under section 244(a)(1) of the former Act. *See Osuchukwu v. INS*, 744 F2d 1136 (5th Cir. 1984). Extreme hardship is a flexible term that depends on the particular facts and circumstances of each case. *See Matter of Hwang*, 10 I&N Dec. 448 (BIA 1964).

The leading case regarding extreme hardship for suspension of deportation applications is *Matter of Anderson*, 16 I&N Dec. 596 (BIA 1978). The BIA identified hardship factors in *Matter of Anderson* that relate to the individual applying for relief. However, hardship to the applicant for a 212(h) waiver is not directly relevant. *Matter of Shaughnessy*, 12 I&N Dec. 810 (BIA 1968). Therefore, it is necessary to examine the effect of deportation or removal on the applicant's qualifying family members to determine whether something other than the ordinary hardship of deportation or removal will occur.

The 212(h) waiver is not only limited to specific grounds of inadmissibility. The circumstances in which the waiver is appropriate are also limited. The BIA has recognized the use of the 212(h) waiver in the following situations:

1) when an alien is an applicant for admission to the United States; or
2) in deportation or removal proceedings:
   a. to waive a ground of inadmissibility that renders an alien deportable on a *nunc pro tunc* (legalese meaning now for then) basis;
   b. in conjunction with an application for adjustment of status under section 245 of the Act; or
   c. in conjunction with an application for registry under section 249 of the Act.

Matter of Sanchez, 17 I&N Dec. 218, 222-23 (BIA 1980); *Matter of*

Parodi, 17 I&N Dec. 608, 611 (BIA 1980); *Matter of Bernabella*, 13 I&N Dec. 42, 44 (BIA 1968).

The 11th Circuit Court of Appeals expanded the availability of the 212(h) waiver in deportation proceedings under the *nunc pro tunc* criteria, regardless of whether or not the applicant had departed from the United States and returned. *Yeung v. INS*, 61 F.3d 833 (11th Cir. 1995). According to *Yeung v. INS*, an alien who is subject to a deportation charge and is otherwise eligible can apply for a 212(h) waiver as long as a qualifying family member exists. Since *Yeung v. INS* was decided using the same rationale as *Francis v. INS*, 532 F.2d 268 (2nd Cir. 1976) (allowing *nunc pro tunc* application of the 212(c) waiver in deportation proceedings), the statutory counterpart rationale (i.e. determining whether an exclusion ground that is comparable or parallel to the charged deportation ground exists) would ordinarily come into play. However as discussed above in connection with the 212(c) waiver, the United States Supreme Court has disapproved the statutory counterpart rationale. *Judulang v. Holder*, 132 S. Ct. 476 (2011). It appears, in the light of these decisions that the 212(h) waiver will become more widely applicable in the near future.

Ineligible Aliens

The following aliens are not eligible for a 212(h) waiver due to limitations on the consent of the Attorney General to an application or reapplication for a visa, admission to the United States, or adjustment of status:

1) aliens who have been convicted of or have admitted to committing acts of murder or torture, or an attempt or conspiracy to commit murder or torture;
2) lawful permanent resident aliens if after the date of admission as a lawful permanent resident the applicant has been convicted for an aggravated felony;

APPROACHING THE BENCH FROM INSIDE THE IMMIGRATION COURT

3) lawful permanent resident aliens who have not resided continuously in the United States for at least 7 years immediately preceding the initiation of deportation or removal proceedings; or

4) aliens who are inadmissible under section 212(a)(2) of the Act (criminal grounds) in cases involving "violent or dangerous crimes."

See section 212(h)(2) of the Act; 8 C.F.R. § 1212.7(d).

In the case of aliens who are inadmissible for "violent and dangerous crimes," consent to apply or reapply for a visa, admission to the United States, or adjustment of status can be given if:

1) the applicant demonstrates "extraordinary circumstances, such as those involving national security or foreign policy considerations;" or

2) denial of such consent would result in "exceptional and extremely unusual hardship."

See 8 C.F.R. § 1212.7(d). This regulation further states that, depending on the gravity of the applicant's offense, "a showing of extraordinary circumstances might still be insufficient to warrant a favorable exercise of discretion under section 212(h)(2) of the Act."

The vague manner in which 8 C.F.R. § 1212.7(d) was drafted and its contents make it almost impossible to refrain from comment. The most obvious observation is that the "exceptional and extremely unusual hardship" standard for consent to consider a 212(h) waiver application is a higher standard than the "extreme hardship" standard for the 212(h) waiver itself. This raises the question of whether the regulatory scheme is inconsistent with the statute by denying access to the waiver by imposing a higher hardship standard than the statutory standard for relief. More than one appellate court has answered this question in the negative by distinguishing between section 212(h)(1) and 212(h)(2) of the Act and emphasizing the broad discretion of the Attorney General regarding consent under the latter section of law. *Samuels v. Chertoff*, 550 F.3d 252, at 257 (2nd Cir. 2008); *Perez Pimental v. Mukasey*, 530 F.3d 321, at 324-25 (5th Cir. 2008); *Mejia v. Gonzalez*, 499 F.3d 991 (9th Cir. 2007). Nevertheless, the result of these decisions appears to be that a regulation bars access to the 212(h) waiver by imposing a higher hardship standard than Congress imposed for relief under section 212(h)(1)(B) of the Act. The tension between the regulation and the statute seems to linger after all the legal reasoning is done. The remaining questions about the application of 8 C.F.R. § 1212.7(d) that remain puzzling to me are:

1) What criteria should be used to classify a crime as a "violent or dangerous crime?"
2) Since a conviction is not necessary for inadmissibility under section 212(a)(2) of the Act, and there might not be any criminal record, what evidence can be considered to classify an offense as a "violent and dangerous crime?"
3) Since section 212(h)(2) of the Act is independent and distinct from section 212(h)(1) of the Act, is it appropriate to limit consideration of hardship to the qualifying relatives identified in the latter section of law? If not, what individuals should be considered for the purpose of determining exceptional and extremely unusual hardship to obtain consent to apply or reapply for a visa, admission to the United States or adjustment of status; the respondent, any family member, any person?
4) What is the scope of "extraordinary circumstances," other than national security or foreign policy considerations?

Perhaps, the reader can think of other unanswered questions about the application of 8 C.F.R. § 1212.7(d).

Another puzzle about the application of section 212(h)(2) of the Act is that Congress appears to have placed a higher burden on lawful permanent residents than on other aliens. For example, a lawful permanent resident who has been convicted for an aggravated felony or has not resided continuously in the United States for 7 years immediately preceding the initiation of immigration court proceedings is not eligible for a 212(h) waiver. However, an alien who entered the United States without inspection or is otherwise unlawfully in the United States and has been convicted for the same aggravated felony remains eligible to apply for a 212(h) waiver (if otherwise eligible) without any residence requirements. Nobody, including DHS attorneys with whom I have discussed this issue, has been able to come up with a cogent explanation.

There has been some litigation generated by unsuccessful attempts to deny "lawful" permanent resident status to gain access to the 212(h) waiver. *See Matter of Ayala-Arevalo*, 22 I&N Dec. 398 (BIA 1998). In *Matter of Ayala-Arevalo*, the respondent asserted that he was not subject to the 7 year continuous residence requirement. According to Ayala-Arevalo, he was inadmissible to the United States on the date he was admitted as a lawful permanent resident because at that time he was involved in an ongoing conspiracy to commit fraud. Therefore, Ayala-Arevalo argued that he was not a *lawful* permanent resident and should not be precluded from applying for relief under section 212(h) of the Act.

Finally, at least three circuit courts have further muddied the water surrounding the 212(h) waiver by holding that aliens who acquire lawful permanent residence through adjustment of status, as opposed to aliens admitted at a port of entry with an immigrant visa, are not barred from applying for relief under section 212(h) of the Act. *Martinez v. Mukasey*, 519 F.3d 532, 544-45 (5th Cir. 2008); *Sum v. Holder*, 602 F.3d 1092, 1096 (9th Cir. 2010); *Lanier v. United States Attorney General*, 631 F.3d 1361, 1366-67 (11th Cir. 2011). The underlying rationale for these decisions is that adjustment of status is not an admission as defined under section 101(a)(13) of the Act. As pointed out by the BIA, if an adjusted alien has not been *admitted* as a lawful permanent resident of the United States an alien who entered the United States without inspection and then adjusted to lawful permanent resident status would not be eligible to apply for a waiver under section 212(c) of the former Act or cancellation of removal for lawful permanent residents under section 240A(a) of the Act because such alien was never *admitted. See Matter of Rosas*, 22 I&N Dec. 616, at 623 (BIA 1999). The BIA continues to adhere to the assimilation approach to adjustment of status (i.e. an applicant for adjustment of status is assimilated to the position of an applicant for admission) and does not follow the rulings of the above cited circuit courts outside of their respective jurisdictions. *Matter of Koljenovic*, 25 I&N Dec. 219 (BIA 2010).

Exercise of Discretion

First as a threshold matter, an applicant for a 212(h) waiver must establish extreme hardship to one or more qualifying relatives if applying under section 212(h)(1)(B) of the Act. *In re Jose Mendez Moralez*, 21 I&N Dec. 296 (BIA 1996). *See Bugayong v. INS*, 442 F.3d 67, at 73 (2nd Cir. 2006). Once an applicant establishes statutory eligibility for a 212(h) waiver, the waiver application may be granted or denied in the exercise of discretion. The exercise of discretion under section 212(h) of the Act requires balancing equities against adverse factors. *In re Mendez-Moralez*, 21 I&N Dec. 296 (BIA 1996).

Favorable factors have been found to include:

1) family ties in the United States, including the quality of such ties (e.g. equity of a marriage and hardship to spouse diminished if parties marry during immigration court proceedings knowing that the applicant might be deported);
2) residence of long duration in the United States, especially when residence began at a young age, including the nature of the applicant's presence (e.g. diminished significance of residence marked by imprisonment);
3) hardship of deportation or removal on the applicant and his or her family;
4) service in the armed forces of the United States;

APPROACHING THE BENCH FROM INSIDE THE IMMIGRATION COURT

5) stable employment history;
6) property and business ties in the United States;
7) value and service to the community;
8) Genuine rehabilitation (Absence of evidence of rehabilitation is not an adverse factor, but absence of rehabilitation is potentially determinative, especially in the presence of serious misconduct and questions about possible reversion to criminal conduct.); and
9) good character.

Adverse factors have been found to include:

1) the nature and circumstances of the exclusion ground relating to the applicant;
2) the nature, recency, an seriousness of the criminal record if it exists; and
3) evidence of bad character.

In re Jose Mendez-Moralez, supra at 299-302.

Once extreme hardship to a qualifying relative is established (see suspension of deportation worksheet for hardship factors), the following worksheet might be useful for identifying the discretionary factors relevant to a 212(h) waiver.

WILLIAM K. ZIMMER

212(h) Waiver Worksheet

I. Family Ties:

II. Length of Residence:

III. Hardship to Applicant:

IV. Hardship to Applicant's Family:

V. Service in the United States Armed Forces:

VI.   Employment History:

VII. Property and Business Ties:

APPROACHING THE BENCH FROM INSIDE THE IMMIGRATION COURT

VIII. Service to the Community:

IX. Rehabilitation:

X. Character:

XI. Nature of Exclusion Ground:

XII. Immigration History:

XIII. Criminal History:

	Cause#	Crime	Commission Date	Conviction Date	Location	Court Disposition
1)						
2)						
3)						
4)						
5)						
6)						

Waiver Under Section 212(i) of the Act

Section 212(i) of the Act provides a waiver for fraud that gives rise to a ground of inadmissibility under section 212(a)(6)(C)(i) of the Act. Before addressing the 212(i) waiver, it is important to understand the elements required to establish inadmissibility for fraud. Not every misrepresentation will support inadmissibility under section 212(a)(6)(C)(i) of the Act. Obviously, if there is no ground of inadmissibility there is no need to qualify for the 212(i) waiver.

Congress established a ground of inadmissibility based on fraud or misrepresentation of a material fact. See section 212(a)(6)(C)(i) of the Act. This section of law requires four elements of proof:

1) misrepresentation or concealment of a fact;
2) the misrepresentation or concealment must be willful;
3) the fact must be material; and
4) the misrepresentation or concealment must be aimed at obtaining a visa, documentation or entry to the United States.

The United States Supreme Court determined in the context of an action to revoke citizenship that a material misrepresentation requires evidence that the misrepresentation either resulted in the erroneous grant of a benefit, or that it had a "natural tendency" to affect the decision to grant the benefit. *Kungys v. United States*, 485 U.S. 759 (1988).

The Attorney General of the United States described the following test for materiality. A misrepresentation made in connection with an application for visa or other documents, or entry into the United States is material if:

1) the alien is inadmissible on the true facts; or
2) the misrepresentation tends to shut off a line of inquiry that is relevant to the alien's eligibility for such visa, other documents, or entry to the United States, and might have resulted in a proper determination of exclusion.

Matter of S- and B-C-, 9 I&N Dec. 436, 447 (A.G. 1961). The BIA

APPROACHING THE BENCH FROM INSIDE THE IMMIGRATION COURT

followed *Matter of S- and B-C-* in *Matter of Bosuego*, 17 I&N Dec. 125 (BIA 1980).

Once a relevant line of inquiry has been shut off and might have resulted in a proper determination of exclusion, the burden of persuasion and proof shifts to the alien to demonstrate that no proper finding of inadmissibility can be made. *Matter of Bosuego, supra; Matter of S- and B-C-, supra. See Kungys v. INS, supra*, at 771-72.

Sometimes, an alien will make a willful misrepresentation of a fact or conceal a fact that the alien thinks is material, but as a matter of law the fact is not material. An example of this is the BIA determination that concealment of minor children, as well as marital status, in a visa application was willful, but not material. *Matter of M-R-*, 9 I&N Dec. 602 (BIA 1962); *Matter of J-D-D-*, 9 I&N Dec. 636 (BIA 1962). The key to analysis with regard to materiality of a misrepresentation or concealment is to answer the following three questions:

1) Does the record establish that the alien is inadmissible based on the true facts? If it does, then the representation was material. If it does not, then the following two questions must be considered.

2) Did the misrepresentation or concealment tend to shut off a line of inquiry that is relevant to the alien's eligibility for a visa, other documents, or admission to the United States? A remote tenuous or fanciful connection between a misrepresentation or concealment and a line of inquiry relevant to eligibility is not sufficient to establish materiality.

3) If a line of inquiry has actually been cut off, might that inquiry have resulted in a proper determination that the alien be excluded from the United States? The alien must carry the burden of persuasion and proof regarding this question.

Matter of J-D-D-, at 688.

If the true facts do not establish inadmissibility in the answer to the first question the following two questions will probably be answered in the alien's favor.

For a misrepresentation or concealment to be willful, the misrepresentation must only be intentional or knowing. Intent to deceive is not necessary to establish a willful misrepresentation or concealment. *Matter of Kai Hing Hui*, 15 I&N Dec. 288 (BIA 1975).

To qualify for a waiver under section 212(i) of the Act, an applicant must:

1) be an immigrant who is the spouse, son, or daughter of a United States citizen or lawful permanent resident of the United States; and
2) establish that refusal of admission would result in extreme hardship to the United States citizen or lawful permanent resident spouse or parent of the applicant.

It is important to note that the qualifying relatives for whom hardship can be considered in connection with a 212(i) waiver are different than the qualifying relatives recognized for suspension of deportation or cancellation of removal for nonpermanent residents and the 212(h) waiver. I have seen applications for a 212(i) waiver that identify a child or son or daughter of a United States citizen or lawful permanent resident of the United States. These applications were not viable for failure to identify a United States citizen or lawful permanent resident *spouse or parent*.

The BIA held that the standard for determining extreme hardship regarding a 212(i) waiver is the same standard used for determining extreme hardship regarding suspension of deportation applications. *Matter of Kao & Lin*, 23 I&N Dec. 45 (BIA 2001). Therefore precedent decisions relating to suspension of deportation applications and the hardship factors discussed above with regard to suspension of deportation are likely to be persuasive authority for consideration of 212(i) waivers.

The BIA has identified the following factors to be considered when making extreme hardship determinations in connection with 212(i) applications:

1) the family ties of qualifying relative(s) to United States citizens or lawful permanent residents of the United States;
2) the family ties of qualifying relative(s) outside the United States;
3) conditions in the country or countries to which the qualifying relative(s) would relocate and the extent of the ties to such country or countries of the qualifying relative(s);
4) the financial impact of departure from the United States; and
5) significant health conditions, especially when tied to the unavailability of suitable medical care in the country to which the qualifying relative(s) would relocate.

Matter of Cervantes-Gonzalez, 22 I&N Dec. 560 (BIA 1999).

Discretion

Once an applicant establishes statutory eligibility for a waiver under section 212(i) of the Act, the waiver may be granted or denied in the exercise of discretion. *Matter of Cervantes, supra.* Like the 212(h) waiver, establishing extreme hardship does not guarantee success for a 212(i) waiver applicant.

According to the BIA, the original purpose of the 212(i) waiver is family unification and the avoidance of the hardship of separation. *Matter of Lopez-Monzon*, 17 I&N Dec. 280, at 281 (BIA 1979). The BIA has identified the following favorable discretionary factors:

1) a viable marriage to a United States citizen;
2) the hardship of separation; and
3) the economic hardship of separation.

Matter of Da Silva, 17 I&N Dec. 288 (BIA 1979).

The Immigration Judge is authorized to consider the underlying fraud or misrepresentation for which the applicant is seeking a 212(i) waiver as an adverse factor in the exercise of discretion when adjudicating this waiver. *Matter of Tijam*, 22 I&N Dec. 408 (BIA 1998); *Matter of Cervantes-Gonzalez, supra.*

The following worksheet might be useful for identifying the discretionary factors relevant to a 212(h) waiver.

APPROACHING THE BENCH FROM INSIDE THE IMMIGRATION COURT
212(i) Worksheet

I. Family Ties of Qualifying Relatives in the United States:

II. Family Ties of Qualifying Relatives Outside the United States:

III. Conditions in the Country or Countries of Relocation:

IV. Ties of Qualifying Relative(s) to Country or Countries of Relocation:

V. Financial Impact of Departure:

VI. Health of the Qualifying Relative(s):

VII. Access to Health Care For the Qualifying Relative:

VIII. Other Hardship to Qualifying Relative(s):

IX. Adverse Factors (e.g. nature and seriousness of applicant's fraud):

Once extreme hardship to a qualifying relative is established, all the factors identified above, including hardship to the applicant are relevant to the exercise of discretion.

Waiver of Invalid Immigrant Document Under Section 212(k) of the Act

An alien who is inadmissible under sections 212(a)(7)(A)(i) of the Act (lack of valid immigrant entry document) and/or 212(a)(5)(A) of the Act (lack of valid labor certificate) can apply for a waiver under section 212(k) of the Act.

To qualify for a 212(k) waiver, the applicant:

1) must be in possession of an immigrant visa;
2) must be otherwise admissible to the United States (i.e. not inadmissible under section 212(a) of the Act for some other ground); and
3) the reason for the invalidity of the applicant's immigrant visa must not have been known to the applicant and not discoverable by reasonable diligence before departure (if the applicant is arriving from an noncontiguous country) or before application for admission to the United States (if the applicant is arriving from a contiguous country).

This waiver can be renewed before an Immigration Judge after denial by the DHS. See 8 C.F.R. § 1212.10. However, an Immigration Judge may make an initial adjudication in immigration court proceedings. *Matter of Aurelio*, 19 I&N Dec. 458 (BIA 1987). Governing regulations provide for the use of a 212(k) waiver in conjunction with adjustment of status under section 245 of the Act. *See* 8 C.F.R. § 1245.1(f).

Once an applicant establishes statutory eligibility for a 212(k) waiver, the Immigration Judge may grant or deny the waiver in the exercise of discretion.

Matter of Aurelio, supra, provides an example of the conditions under which the need for a waiver might arise. In *Matter of Aurelio,* the United States State Department had issued an immigrant visa to the applicant who was the beneficiary of an immigrant visa petition (as the daughter of a United States Citizen) filed by her United States citizen father. The applicant's father died after a lengthy illness more than 1 year before the immigrant visa was issued and the applicant's departure from the Philippines. Unfortunately for the applicant, the BIA dismissed her appeal upon agreeing with the Immigration Judge that she had not demonstrated the reason for her invalid immigrant visa was not discoverable by reasonable diligence before her departure from the Philippines.

The applicant in *Matter of Aurelio,* had been placed in exclusion proceedings which is the equivalent of a respondent charged as an arriving alien in removal proceedings. Former governing regulations authorized Immigration Judges to consider 212(k) waivers in deportation proceedings as well as exclusion proceedings. *See* 8 C.F.R. § 242.8(a) (1987). *Matter of Aurelio, supra.*

Chapter VIII
Voluntary Departure

There have always been two versions of voluntary departure; voluntary return or pre-hearing voluntary departure, and voluntary departure at the conclusion of immigration proceedings. Before the passage of IIRIRA on September 30, 1996, voluntary return was exclusively administered and executed by agents and officers of the former INS. *See* section 244(a)(1) of the former Act. Even after deportation proceedings were initiated, the respondent and trial attorney could independently agree to a voluntary return. If this occurred the former INS or both parties would move to terminate deportation proceedings which would usually be granted in deference to the prosecutorial discretion of the INS. If the respondent asked for voluntary departure at the conclusion of deportation proceedings the Special Inquiry Officer or Immigration Judge would adjudicate the request and issue a voluntary departure order if granted.

After the passage of IIRIRA, new regulations gave the Immigration Judge authority (for 30 days after the master calendar hearing at which an initial merits hearing is calendared) over voluntary return or pre-hearing voluntary departure. Thus, the Immigration Judge's jurisdiction over pre-hearing voluntary departure now overlaps with the jurisdiction of the DHS. *See* 8 C.F.R. § 1240.26(b)(1)(i), (ii). An alien can also request voluntary departure from the DHS before initiation of removal proceedings *See* 8 C.F.R. § 240.25.

Generally, the only advantage of voluntary departure to the alien is the opportunity to depart from the United States without being taken into custody and elimination of the need for special permission to return within a specified number of years and criminal sanctions for attempting to return or returning to the United States without permission during the specified time bar. *See* section 212(a)(9)(A) of the Act.

Voluntary Departure Before IIRIRA

To qualify for voluntary departure in deportation proceedings (immigration proceedings initiated before the passage of IIRIRA by filing an Order to Show Cause (Form I-221)) an applicant must demonstrate that:

1) the applicant is and has been a person of good moral character for at least 5 years preceding the application; and
2) the applicant has the immediate means with which to depart promptly from the United States.

See section 244(e) of the former Act; 8 C.F.R. § 240.49(b) (1995).

An applicant who is subject to deportation under sections 241(a) (2) (criminal grounds), (3) (failure to register under section 265 of the Act; convictions for failure to register under section 266 of the Act; violation of section 36(c) of the Alien Registration Act of 1940; violation of the Foreign Agents Registration Act (22 U.S.C. 611 et seq.); violations of 18 U.S.C. 1546 (visa and document fraud); or subject to final order for civil document fraud)), or (4) (security, terrorist, foreign policy, or Nazi persecution grounds) of the former Act is not eligible for voluntary departure, unless the applicant has been physically present in the United States for a continuous period of at least 10 years following the event or circumstance that gave rise to a deportation ground under the above described sections of law. *Matter of Risco*, 20 I&N Dec. 109, at 111 (BIA 1989).

APPROACHING THE BENCH FROM INSIDE THE IMMIGRATION COURT

All of the pre-IIRIRA voluntary departure applications involving the 10 year continuous physical presence requirement that I have considered during my work in the former INS and in EOIR were based on criminal convictions rather than any of the other grounds that trigger the 10 year continuous physical presence requirement. Since the date of the criminal conviction marks the event or circumstance underlying the deportation ground, calculating 10 years from such date was relatively simple.

Failure to Depart

If an alien fails to depart within the time allowed for voluntary departure granted in deportation proceedings in the absence of exceptional circumstances the alien will become ineligible for a period of 5 years for:

1) voluntary departure under section 244(e) of the former Act;
2) suspension of deportation under section 244(a)(1) of the former Act;
3) adjustment of status under sections 245 (immigrant) and 248 (nonimmigrant) of the Act; and
4) Registry under section 249 of the Act.

See section 242B(e)(2)(A) of the former Act. *Matter of Shaar*, 21 I&N Dec. 541 (BIA 1996) *aff'd, Shaar v. INS*, 141 F.3d 953 (9th Cir. 1998).

Voluntary Departure Subsequent to IIRIRA
Prior to Conclusion of Removal Proceedings

To qualify for voluntary departure *at the applicant's own expense* under section 240B(a) of the Act (prior to conclusion of removal proceedings), an applicant must:

1) request voluntary departure at or before a master calendar hearing;
2) make no other requests for relief;
3) concede that the applicant is subject to removal;
4) waive appeal on all issues;
5) present a passport or travel document to the DHS for inspection and copying within 60 days of the order granting voluntary departure;
6) have not been convicted of an aggravated felony under section 101(a)(43) of the Act; and
7) not be subject to deportation under section 237(a)(4) of the Act (security and related grounds).

See 8 C.F.R. § 1240.26(b)(1)(i)

Limitations

Voluntary departure prior to conclusion of removal proceedings is subject to the following limitations:

1) The period of time in which an alien may be allowed to depart voluntarily cannot exceed 120 days. *See* section 240B(a)(2) of the Act.
2) An alien may be required to post a voluntary departure bond to ensure departure within the time permitted. *See* section 240B(a)(3) of the Act.
3) An Immigration Judge may not grant voluntary departure if 30 days have passed after the master calendar hearing at which a merits hearing (presumably a final hearing on relief) is initially calendared; and
4) An Immigration Judge may impose other conditions deemed necessary to ensure timely departure.

Miscellaneous

The BIA set forth a good description of voluntary departure requirements and a comparison of pre-hearing and post-hearing voluntary departure in *Matter of Arguelles-Campos*, 22 I&N Dec. 811 (BIA 1999). For example, an applicant need not establish good moral character to qualify for voluntary departure prior to the conclusion of removal proceedings. *Matter of Arguelles-Campos*, at 816; *Matter of Cordova*, 22 I&N Dec. 966 (BIA 1999). The DHS attorney has the authority to stipulate to pre-hearing voluntary departure at any time prior to the conclusion of removal proceedings, regardless of the expiration of the Immigration Judge's jurisdiction 30 days after the last master calendar hearing. Also, a grant of voluntary departure does not guarantee release from custody. *Matter of M-A-S-*, 24 I&N Dec. 762 (BIA 2009).

There appears to be potential for uncertainty and, therefore, controversy about the definition of master calendar hearings and merits hearings in connection with the jurisdiction of the Immigration Judge over voluntary departure prior to conclusion of removal proceedings. Definitions of "master calendar hearing" and "merits hearing" do not exist anywhere in statute or regulation. Removal hearings are sometimes postponed to address issues over the DHS allegations and charges that involve the submission of evidence and testimony (e.g. controversy over an alleged unlawful entry or derivative citizenship). Is this a "merits hearing" contemplated in 8 C.F.R. § 1240.26(b)(1)(ii)? Sometimes, a case previously scheduled for a merits hearing is rescheduled as a master calendar hearing when the new potential for additional relief becomes apparent (e.g. the filing of a visa petition by a United States citizen who is an immediate relative, the emergence of a new qualifying relative by marriage or birth, the discovery of a medical or psychological condition that requires testing and evaluation, etc.). Sometimes cases are rescheduled as a different type of hearing for administrative reasons without consulting the parties. It appears that the key phrase regarding Immigration Judge jurisdiction when merits hearings are rescheduled as master calendar hearings is "the master calendar hearing at which the case is *initially* calendared for a merits hearing" (emphasis added). *See* 8 C.F.R. § 1240.26(b)(1)(ii). Nevertheless, without a definition for "master calendar hearing" and "merits hearing," the stage is set for legal wrangling.

At Conclusion of Removal Proceedings

To qualify for voluntary departure at the conclusion of removal proceedings, an applicant must demonstrate that:

1) the applicant has been physically present in the United States for at least 1 year immediately preceding service of the Notice to Appear;
2) the applicant is and has been a person of good moral character for at least 5 years preceding the application for voluntary departure;
3) the applicant has not been convicted for an aggravated felony defined under section 101(a)(43) of the Act and is not subject to deportation for security or terrorist related grounds under section 237(a)(4) of the Act; and
4) the applicant, based on clear and convincing evidence, has the means to depart and intends to do so.

See section 240B(b)(1) of the Act.

Limitations

Voluntary departure at the conclusion of removal proceedings is subject to the following limitations:

1) The period of time in which an alien may be allowed to depart at the conclusion of removal proceedings cannot exceed 60 days. *See* section 240B(b)(2) of the Act.

APPROACHING THE BENCH FROM INSIDE THE IMMIGRATION COURT

2) An alien who is permitted to depart at the conclusion of removal proceedings must post a voluntary departure bond in an amount necessary to ensure departure. *See* section 240B(b)(3) of the Act.

3) An applicant must present a travel document sufficient to assure lawful entry to the country to which the alien is departing. *See* 8 C.F.R. § 1240.26(c)(2).

4) The required bond must be at least $500 and must be posted within 5 business days of the order granting voluntary departure. *See* 8 C.F.R. § 1240.26(c)(3).

Ineligible Aliens

An alien who has previously been granted voluntary departure after having been found inadmissible for being present in the United States without admission or parole under section 212(a)(6)(A) of the Act is not eligible for voluntary departure prior to conclusion of removal proceedings as well as voluntary departure at the conclusion of removal proceedings. *See* section 240B(c) of the Act. An alien who was allowed to voluntarily depart without the institution of immigration court proceedings has not been "found inadmissible" under section 240 of the Act. In my experience, such alien is deemed eligible for voluntary departure, even though he or she had previously been granted voluntary departure by the DHS. The BIA has held that an alien granted multiple voluntary departures under section 244(c) of the former Act was not barred from voluntary departure in removal proceedings because the alien had not been granted voluntary departure under section 240B of the Act. *Matter of Arguelles-Campos*, 22 I&N Dec. 811, at 818 (BIA 1999).

Failure to Depart

If an alien fails to voluntarily depart within the time allowed for voluntary departure granted in removal proceedings the alien will become subject to a civil penalty of at least $1000, but not more than $5000, and will become ineligible for a period of 10 years for:

1) Voluntary departure under section 240B of the Act;
2) Cancellation of removal under section 240A(b) of the Act;
3) Adjustment of status under sections 245 (immigrants) and 248 (nonimmigrants) of the Act; and
4) Registry under section 249 of the Act.

See section 240B(d) of the Act.

There is an exception for battered spouses and children if extreme cruelty or battery was at least one central reason for failure to depart. *See* section 240B(d)(2) of the Act.

Unilateral Withdrawal of Voluntary Departure

The United States Supreme Court determined that voluntary departure is a *quid pro quo* (legalese meaning "this for that") agreement between an alien and the United States government, and that an alien who has entered into a voluntary departure agreement has the option of unilaterally withdrawing his or her agreement before the expiration of the time allowed for voluntary departure. *Dada v. Mukasey*, 554 U.S. 1 (2008). The fundamental rationale behind *Dada v. Mukasey* is to protect an alien's right to file a motion to reopen immigration proceedings.

As noted above, voluntary departure avoids the consequences of a deportation or removal order as well as being taken into federal custody for removal. Therefore, unilateral withdrawal of a voluntary departure agreement triggers specific consequences under governing regulations. Specifically, if an alien files a motion to reopen or a motion to reconsider *during the period allowed* for

APPROACHING THE BENCH FROM INSIDE THE IMMIGRATION COURT

voluntary departure it is deemed a unilateral withdrawal of the voluntary departure agreement. Therefore, the voluntary departure benefit will terminate automatically and the alternative order of removal will immediately take effect. *See* 8 C.F.R. §§ 1240.26(b)(3)(iii) and 1240.26I(1). Filing a motion to reopen or a motion to reconsider *after* the time allowed for voluntary departure has expired, even if granted, will not in any way alter the period of time allowed for voluntary departure and does not vacate or vitiate the penalties for failure to depart, except for battered spouses and children under section 240B(d)(2) of the Act. *See* 8 C.F.R. §§ 1240.26(e)(2) and 1240.26(f).

Chapter IX
Bond Hearings

Section 236 of the Act provides for the arrest, detention, and release of aliens who are subject to removal from the United States. *See* 8 C.F.R. § 1236.1. Congress mandated the detention of criminal aliens identified as follows:

1) aliens inadmissible for commission of any offense described in section 212(a)(2) of the Act (criminal grounds for inadmissibility);
2) aliens deportable for the commission of any offense described in section 237(a)(2)(A)(ii) (multiple criminal convictions), (A)(iii) (aggravated felony), (B) (convictions relating to controlled substances), (C) (firearms convictions), or (D) (conspiracies or attempts to commit any offense relating to espionage, sabotage, treason or sedition);
3) aliens deportable under section 237(a)(2)(A)(i) (crimes involving moral turpitude) based on an offense for which the alien has been sentenced to at least 1 year; or
4) aliens inadmissible under section 212(a)(3)(B) of the Act or deportable under section 237(a)(4)(B) of the Act (terrorist activities).

Congress limited the release of the above described criminal aliens under conditions set forth in section 236(c)(2) of the Act. If the plain language of section 236(c)(2) is applied, aliens described in section

236(c)(1) of the Act can only be released from DHS custody when the release is necessary to protect witnesses, potential witnesses, or persons cooperating with investigations of major criminal activity and if the released alien will not pose a danger to the safety of other persons or property and if the alien is likely to appear for any scheduled immigration proceedings. This severely limits the release of most criminal aliens, including lawful permanent residents.

On September 30, 1996, Congress issued transition period custody rules ("TPCR") that expired on October 1, 1998. *See* section 303(b)(3) of Div. C of Pub. L. 104-208. Under the TPCR, the DHS can generally release lawful permanent residents, except for aliens who are inadmissible or deportable for terrorist activities, so long as they will not pose a danger to the safety of other persons or property and are likely to appear for any scheduled hearing. Congress also provided for the release of aliens not lawfully admitted to the United States, who cannot be removed due to refusal of the designated country of removal to accept them. An example of a country that has refused repatriation is Cuba.

The result of the restrictive release criteria in section 236(c)(2) of the Act and the promulgation of the TPCR is a string of BIA decisions and court decisions containing seemingly strained rationales for applying the TPCR standards for release after the expiration of the TPCR. *See Matter of Garcia Arreola*, 25 I&N Dec. 267 (BIA 2010). The BIA, in *Matter of Garcia Arreola*, held that mandatory detention of a criminal alien under section 236(c) of the Act is required only if such alien is released from non-DHS custody (e.g. state custody) after the expiration of the TPCR, and only when the alien had been detained in connection with one or more of the grounds described in section 236(c)(1) of the Act at the time of the post-TPCR release. The BIA overruled *Matter of Saysana*, 24 I&N Dec. 602 (BIA 2008) and modified *Matter of Adeniji*, 22 I&N Dec. 1102 (BIA 1999) in arriving at the ultimate holding in *Garcia Arreola*. The BIA noted that the DHS joined the respondent in asking for a more narrow application of section 236(c)(2) of the Act. Detaining aliens is very expensive and imposes a heavy burden on government resources.

The reader might want to review 8 C.F.R. § 1003.19(h)(1)(i) to determine whether an Immigration Judge has authority to redetermine custody conditions for aliens who are taken into the DHS custody. If an alien is eligible for a bond redetermination hearing the following worksheet for organizing factors relevant to immigration custody bonds might be helpful.

WILLIAM K. ZIMMER

Bond Worksheet

I. Biography
- A. Age:
- B. Gender:
- C. Citizenship:
- D. Marital Status:

II. United States Family Ties

                                    USC   LPR   Other

- A. Spouse:

- B. Children:
  - (1) Male:

  - (2) Female:

- C. Mother:

- D. Father:

- E. Siblings:
  - (1) Male:

  - (2) Female:

- F. Other:
  - (1) Uncle(s):

  - (2) Aunt(s):

  - (3) Cousin(s):

  - (4) Nephew(s):

  - (5) Nieces(s):

APPROACHING THE BENCH FROM INSIDE THE IMMIGRATION COURT

(6)   Grandparent(s):

III. Entry
    A.   When:

    B.   How:

IV. Immigration History
    A.   Entries:

    B.   Removals:

    C.   Smuggling:

V. Nature and Viability of Removal Charge

VI. Criminal History

VII. History of Bond Compliance

VIII. Relief From Removal

WILLIAM K. ZIMMER

IX. Residence if Released

X. Property Ties
    A. Real:

    B. Personal:

XI. Work History/Business Ties

XII. Other Miscellaneous Factors

APPROACHING THE BENCH FROM INSIDE THE IMMIGRATION COURT

Bond hearings are separate and apart from other immigration court proceedings. Therefore, evidence submitted at a bond hearing is not part of the record of proceedings for other purposes. For example, if evidence submitted at a bond hearing is material to removal proceedings the party that is sponsoring the evidence must submit it again during removal proceedings. Some attorneys forget about this or overlook it. Finally, bond hearings are relatively informal. There is no official record of bond proceedings. Immigration Judges issue written bond decisions only if a bond appeal is filed. The written decision will be based on the Immigration Judge's notes and the evidence submitted during the bond hearing.

Immigration Judges have different approaches and styles when it comes to conducting bond redetermination hearings. Personally, I preferred not to entertain witnesses. I questioned the attorneys about what I thought was relevant and allowed the attorneys to tell me anything that they thought was important if I didn't ask about it. Given the informal nature of off-the-record bond redetermination hearings and the relatively fast pace at most immigration detention facilities, listening to witnesses in the context of bond redetermination hearings is not ordinarily an efficient use of time. If the attorneys are well prepared the relevant bond factors will be disclosed with a minimal tax on the time of all participants, without affecting the ultimate bond disposition.

Chapter X
Motions to Reopen and Motions to Reconsider

The work description of the Immigration Judge would not be complete without discussing motions to reopen and motions to reconsider. An Immigration Judge must dedicate a significant amount of time to adjudicating motions to reopen and motions to reconsider. These motions are generally the equivalent of a motion for new trial in civil and criminal proceedings. Thus, regulations regarding motions to reopen are framed negatively and authorize reopening only when minimum conditions are met. *INS v. Wang*, 450 U.S. 139 (1981). *See also INS v. Abudu*, 485 U.S. 94 (1988).

Motions to reopen are distinct from motions to reconsider. *Matter of Cerna*, 20 I&N Dec. 399 (BIA 1991). A motion to reopen seeks an opportunity to present new evidence so that a new decision can be entered based on a *new* factual record. *See* 8 C.F.R. § 1003.23(b)(3). *Matter of Cerna, supra.* A motion to reconsider addresses error made at the time the original decision is rendered and seeks re-examination of the *original* factual record in the light of new law or new legal arguments. *See* 8 C.F.R. § 1003.23(b)(2). *Matter of Cerna, supra.* Both motions to reopen and motions to reconsider are limited to final administrative orders of exclusion, deportation, or removal. *See* 8 C.F.R. § 1003.23(b)(1). For example, governing regulations do not provide for motions to reopen or reconsider interlocutory decisions. An interlocutory decision is a decision in immigration proceedings that does not result in a final disposition of proceedings (e.g. a decision relating to a motion to change venue or a motion for adjournment, etc.).

On more than one occasion, I have witnessed motions to reconsider labeled as motions to reopen. Regardless of how a motion was labeled, however, I would address it according to the nature of the motion (i.e. based on what the moving party was seeking).

The reader might recall a brief description of *in absentia* orders in chapter II. There is no appeal allowed in the case of an *in absentia* order. Filing a motion to reopen is the only way to challenge an *in absentia* order. *See* section 240(b)(5)(C) of the Act. Motions to reopen hearings conducted *in absentia* account for a relatively large number of motions filed in immigration court.

The requirements of a motion to reopen and rescind an in absentia removal order are as follows:

1) The motion must be filed within 180 days after the date of the removal order if the alien is seeking to demonstrate exceptional circumstances (defined under section 240(e)(1) of the Act) for failure to appear; or

2) The motion may be filed without any time limit if the alien is seeking to demonstrate insufficient notice under section 239(a)(1) and (2) of the Act.

The filing of a motion to reopen and rescind an *in absentia* removal order stays the removal order while it is pending before the Immigration Judge. It might be helpful to know that if the alien is seeking to demonstrate exceptional circumstances to justify reopening a fee is required. *See* 8 C.F.R. § 1003.24(b)(1). If, however, the alien is seeking to demonstrate insufficient notice no fee is required. *See* 8 C.F.R. § 1003.24(b)(2)(v). If the alien is seeking to demonstrate both exceptional circumstances and insufficient notice, I believe a fee is required under 8 C.F.R. § 1003.24(b)(2)(v). Rejection of a motion by the immigration court because a required fee is

APPROACHING THE BENCH FROM INSIDE THE IMMIGRATION COURT

not paid can result in the removal of an alien between the time of rejection and the time of proper filing. When the DHS deportation officer checks with the immigration court to verify whether a motion to reopen is pending, a computer check will indicate no motion pending. A rejected motion is not pending.

The requirements for motions to reopen hearings conducted in the respondent's presence are as follows:

1) The motion must be filed within 90 days of the date of the final administrative order of removal, deportation, or exclusion, or on or before September 30, 1996, whichever is later.

2) The motion must state whether the validity of the order has been or is the subject of any judicial proceeding, and if so, the nature and date of the proceeding, the court in which the proceeding took place or is pending, and the result or status.

3) The motion must state whether the subject of the order is also the subject of criminal proceedings and the current status of those proceedings.

4) The motion must state the new facts that the moving party is seeking to establish.

5) The motion must be accompanied by affidavits and other evidence.

6) If the motion seeks consideration of an application for relief from removal the motion must be accompanied by the appropriate application and supporting documents, including a fee receipt for such application if required.

7) The motion must establish that the evidence offered is material and was not available or could not have been discovered or presented at the last hearing.

8) If the moving party is seeking consideration of any discretionary relief application the motion must establish that the right to apply for such relief was not fully explained

by the Immigration Judge or that an opportunity to apply for such relief was not afforded during the previous removal proceedings, unless the relief sought is based on circumstances that occurred subsequent to the last hearing.

9) If the moving party is seeking cancellation of removal for lawful permanent residents or for non-permanent residents under sections 240A(a) or 240A(b) of the Act, the motion must establish statutory eligibility for such relief before service of the Notice to Appear or before the commission of the offense that renders the moving party subject to removal.

10) The motion must be accompanied by a fee receipt if a fee is required.

11) The motion must be accompanied by a certificate of service on the opposing party.

See 8 C.F.R. § 1003.23(b)(1), (3) and § 1003.24(b)(1), (c)(2).

The requirements for a motion to reconsider are as follows:

1) The motion must specify the errors of fact or law in the Immigration Judge's previous decision.

2) The motion must be supported by pertinent authority.

3) The motion must be supported by a fee receipt if a fee is required.

4) The motion must be accompanied by a certificate of service on the opposing party.

See 8 C.F.R. § 1003.23(b)(2). *See Matter of O-S-G-*, 24 I&N Dec. 56 (BIA 2006) (discussing a motion to reconsider a BIA decision).

A stay is not automatic for motions to reopen immigration proceedings and motions to reconsider that were conducted in the presence of the respondent or applicant. *See* 8 C.F.R. § 1003.23(b)(1)(v). A determination to grant or deny a stay (if a stay is requested) is, in part, dependent on the strength or likelihood of success of the motion itself. A motion for a stay of removal filed without the underlying motion to reopen or motion to reconsider lacks

APPROACHING THE BENCH FROM INSIDE THE IMMIGRATION COURT

justification for a favorable disposition. According to the United States Supreme Court, the following four factors govern decisions regarding stays of removal:

1) whether the stay applicant has made a strong showing that the applicant is likely to succeed on the merits (e.g. the motion to reopen);
2) whether the stay applicant will be irreparably injured if the stay is denied;
3) whether the issuance of the stay will substantially injure other interested parties in the proceedings; and
4) where the public interest lies.

Nken v. Holder, 566 U.S. 418 (2009).

It is important to note that statements made in a brief or motion are not evidence and are not entitled to evidentiary weight. *INS v. Phinpathya*, 464 U.S. 183, 188-89, n.6 (1989); *Matter of Ramirez-Sanchez*, 17 I&N Dec. 503 (BIA 1980). I have seen motions filed by attorneys representing respondents and attorneys for the DHS that were based solely on raw statements in the motions themselves without supporting evidence.

An Immigration Judge can *sua sponte* (legalese meaning by spontaneous urging or recommendation) reconsider any order or disposition or reopen any proceeding that he or she issued or concluded. The BIA has held that an alien who is seeking the favorable exercise of *sua sponte* authority must demonstrate the existence of an exceptional situation that warrants reopening. *Matter of Beckford*, 22 I&N Dec. 1216 (BIA 2000).

Aside from *sua sponte* reopening and joint motions, the primary exception to time and number bars is a motion to reopen to apply for asylum under section 208 of the Act, withholding of removal under section 241(b)(3) of the Act, or withholding of removal under the Convention Against Torture based on changed circumstances in the country of nationality or the country to which removal has been ordered. However, the changed circumstances must be material and not available or could not have been discovered or presented at the previous hearing. *See* 8 C.F.R. § 1003.23(b)(4). Changes in an alien's personal circumstances (e.g. the birth of children) in the United States will not, without more, justify a motion to reopen to pursue a successive application based on changed circumstances as described in section 208(a)(2)(D) of the Act. *See Wang v. Board of Immigration Appeals*, 437 F.3d 270, 273 (2nd Cir. 2006); *Zheng v. Mukasey*, 509 F.3d 869 (8th Cir. 2007).

A plain reading of the regulations for motions to reopen *in absentia* orders does not clearly authorize reopening based on changed circumstances in the country of nationality or the country to which removal has been ordered, because the focus of reopening *in absentia* orders is justification for failure to appear. *See* 8 C.F.R. § 1003.23(b)(4)(ii), (iii). Nevertheless, the BIA held that changed conditions in the homeland of an applicant for admission to the United States in exclusion proceedings established reasonable cause for reopening an *in absentia* order. *Matter of A-N- & R-M-N-*, 22 I&N Dec. 953 (BIA 1999).

Finally, motions to reopen and to reconsider are subject to time and number bars. Specifically, aliens are limited to only 1 motion to reconsider and only 1 motion to reopen. The DHS, however, is exempt. *See* 8 C.F.R. § 1003.23(b)(1). A motion to reconsider must be filed within 30 days of the date of any final administrative order or on or before July 31, 1996, whichever is later. A motion to reopen must be filed within 90 days of the date of entry of a final administrative order or on or before September 30, 1996, whichever is later. *See* 8 C.F.R. § 1003.23(b)(1). The time bar is different for motions to reopen and rescind *in absentia* orders as described above (i.e. 180 days for motions based on exceptional circumstances for failure to appear and no time limit for motions based on insufficient notice).

Conclusion

In a letter composed approximately in January 1784, Benjamin Franklin wrote in response to an inquiry about conditions relating to resettlement in the United States from Europe:

> Our Country offers to Strangers nothing but a good Climate, fertile Soil, wholesome Air, Free Governments, wise Laws, Liberty, a good People to live among, and a hearty Welcome. Those Europeans who have these or greater Advantages at home, would do well to stay where they are.

See Franklin, pp. 1083-84, copyright 1987 by Literary Classics of the United States, Inc., New York, N.Y. One cannot help but to wonder what Benjamin Franklin would think about the current conditions relating to immigration in the United States.

In 2013, the political atmosphere in the United States is producing storms of debate on the topic of immigration policy. The most recent overhaul of United States immigration law before 2013 occurred on September 30, 1996, when Congress passed the Illegal Immigration Reform and Immigrant Responsibility Act of 1996 ("IIRIRA"). Although IIRIRA is considered by most to be a major change in law, IIRIRA, as well as previous immigration legislation passed subsequent to June 27, 1952, remains rooted in or grafted on the Immigration and Nationality Act of 1952. For example, in spite of eliminating deportation and exclusion proceedings in favor of removal proceedings, Congress retained distinct exclusion and deportation grounds for framing removal charges in the style of the Immigration and Nationality Act of 1952. Although changes in law are necessary to effect changes in policy in response to current domestic political and economic conditions and international developments, it seems obvious that if laws are not enforced they amount to nothing more than printed text on paper.

Regardless of whether the federal government is unwilling or unable to enforce immigration laws aimed at securing the borders of the United States, the result is the same. The current estimate thrown about in the news media is in the range of 11 to 12 million undocumented aliens in the United States (including aliens who were legally admitted for temporary visits, but remained longer than permitted). The reason there are 11 to 12 million undocumented aliens in the United States appears to be the failure of the federal government to enforce the past and current immigration laws. New legislation aimed at securing the United States borders, if not enforced, will not enjoy better success than past and current legislation.

After 35 years of federal service as a customs inspector, immigration attorney and an Immigration Judge, it seems obvious to me that, regardless of what immigration policies Congress commits to legislation, failure to physically secure the borders of the United States will frustrate the purpose of such legislation or otherwise make enforcement impossible. If physically securing the United States borders is not possible, as some have argued, the United States must suffer increased exposure to the very real hazards of a dangerous world and ultimately risk its national identity. The term, "nation without borders," is an oxymoron.

Despite the challenges and dangers facing the United States in connection with immigration policy and border security, the future is bright. The history of the United States informs us that millions of people from other countries want to come to the United States to make a new future in a great bountiful and free nation where individual rights are respected. They bring with them fresh ideas, skills and a positive desire to contribute and become part of the social fabric and economy of the United States to the mutual benefit of themselves and the nation. Illegal immigration may threaten the domestic stability of the United States, but legal immigration strengthens and nourishes and allows control over the flow of immigration consistent with the best interests of United States citizens and lawful permanent residents. Controlled legal immigration aligned with national needs and interests also encourages the assimilation of immigrants into our national tapestry, as opposed to the fabrication of a patchwork of factions nourished by a constant unchecked flow of migration from source countries. It is instructive to consider the opinion of James Madison regarding factions:

> The latent causes of faction are thus sown in the nature of man; and we see them everywhere brought into different degrees of activity, according to the different circumstances of civil society. A zeal for different opinions concerning religion, concerning government, and many other points, as well as speculation as of practice; an attachment of different leaders ambitiously contending for pre-eminence and power; or to persons of other descriptions whose fortunes have been interesting to the human passions, have, in turn, divided mankind into parties, inflamed them with mutual animosity, and rendered them much more disposed to vex and oppress each other than to cooperate for their common good. So strong is this propensity of mankind to fall into mutual animosities, that where no substantial occasion presents itself, the most frivolous and fanciful distinctions have been sufficient to kindle their unfriendly passions and excite their most violent conflicts.

See The Federalist, No. 10. If we agree with Madison's observation of mankind's predilection for forming factions it is important for assimilation of new immigrants to take place for the sake of future civil order. Assimilation into American life may take more than one generation, but it seems more likely to occur naturally if there are ebbs and flows of immigration in response to the national needs and interests of the United States. History teaches that before the Immigration and Nationality Act of 1965 the United States experienced some periods of low volumes of immigration (and even emigration by some groups), especially during World War I (1914 – 1918) and during the Great Depression (beginning in 1929). The following is an excerpt from the *Report of Mr. Dillingham, from the Committee on Immigration, April 28, 1921*:

> It also appears that during the 10 years, 1905-1914, that we admitted 10,121,940 immigrants; that the number admitted during the five years 1915-1919, was almost negligible, while that in the fiscal year 1920 was 430,001, or less than one-half the normal flow before the war.

See U.S. 67th Congress, 1st session, *Senate Report No. 17*, pp. 3-8.

Surely, historic periods of low immigration must have encouraged assimilation of immigrants living in the United States and their absorption into the mainstream of American society. Opening and closing the immigration faucet according to national needs and interests is impossible when uncontrolled illegal immigration is flooding into the United States.

The immigration courts of the United States play a role in maintaining a respectable impression of the United States in the eyes of other nations and international good will by firmly and fairly applying United States immigration law. The manner in which our immigration laws are applied characterizes our government's intimate interactions with the people who inhabit the earth with us in all of its diverse countries. This is true because the application of immigration law affects people on a personal level. Thus, like pixels that comprise a photograph, the work of United States immigration courts projects an image of the United States on a world wide screen through the minds of persons (and through the minds of their families, friends and countrymen) who come before an Immigration Judge. It seems important to the national interest of the United States for the projected image to include fundamental fairness; not just the application of law, but justice seasoned with compassion. Our immigration courts are a window to the world that provides a view of American national character.

The best way to ensure fundamental fairness and the perception of justice seasoned with compassion in United States immigration courts is to strengthen and protect the independent decision making role of Immigration Judges. In addition, only persons of a judicial temperament who possess appropriate people skills should be appointed as Immigration Judges. Vetting candidates seeking appointment as an Immigration Judge for political orientation should absolutely be avoided. The reader might recall the 1911 *Report of the U.S. Immigration Commission* regarding boards of special inquiry in Chapter I. The 1911 *U.S. Immigration Commission* noted in its report that boards of special inquiry "exercise a power which if not properly used may result in injustice to the immigrant or, through the admission of undesirable aliens, in harm to the country." This is a description of the same power presently exercised by Immigration Judges. Therefore, it seems reasonable to conclude that the same qualities the 1911 *U.S. Immigration Commission* deemed important in a special inquiry board member are desirable qualities in an Immigration Judge today. In justice to the immigrant, and to the country as well, the corps of Immigration Judges should be composed of unprejudiced persons of "ability, training, and good judgment" that "fit them for the judicial functions performed." *See Brief Statement of the Investigations of the Immigration Commission, with Conclusions and Recommendations and Views of the Minority, Reports of the U.S. Immigration Commission (1911).* Any organization is only as good as the people who are in it.

Hopefully, the history of the immigration law and the Immigration Judge and discussion about the ordinary daily work that United States Immigration Judges perform have imparted insight about the institutions assigned to enforce, adjudicate and administer immigration law in the United States. United States immigration courts are a unique feature of our government that distinguishes the United States from most other countries with regard to procedures for resolving controversies arising from the application of immigration laws and policies. United States immigration courts reflect the United States government's dedication to due process and respect for the constitutional and legal rights of individuals who are subject to the sovereign authority of the United States to determine, consistent with our national interests, what aliens should be admitted, excluded, or deported. These unique administrative courts need to be independent to credibly carry out the judicial role to which they have been assigned.

Puck: If we shadows have offended,
Think but this, and all is mended –
That you have but slumb'red here
While these visions did appear.
And this weak and idle theme,
No more yielding but a dream,
Gentles, do no reprehend.
If you pardon, we will mend.
And, as I am an honest Puck,
If we have unearned luck
Now to escape the serpent's tongue,
We will make amends ere long;
Else the Puck a liar call.
So good night unto you all.
Give me your hands, if we be friends,
And Robin shall restore amends.

William Shakespeare
Midsummer Night's Dream – Act V – Scene 2